The United States and the Global Environment

A guide to American organizations concerned with international environmental issues

Edited by
Thaddeus C. Trzyna
with the assistance of
Nancy Matsumoto

California Institute of Public Affairs
An Affiliate of The Claremont Colleges

WHO'S DOING WHAT SERIES: 9

The United States
and the Global Environment

A Guide to American Organizations Concerned with
International Environmental Issues

Edited by
THADDEUS C. TRZYNA

with the assistance of
NANCY MATSUMOTO

CALIFORNIA INSTITUTE OF PUBLIC AFFAIRS
An Affiliate of The Claremont Colleges

Published and distributed by the California Institute of
Public Affairs, P.O. Box 10, Claremont, California 91711,
Telephone (714) 624-5212.

Library of Congress Cataloging in Publication Data
Main entry under title:

The United States and the global environment.

    (Who's doing what series ; 9)
    Includes index.
    1. Environmental protection--Societies, etc.--
Directories. 2. Conservation of natural resources--
Societies, etc.--Directories. I. Trzyna, Thaddeus C.,
1939-   . II. Matsumoto, Nancy. III. Series.
TD169.6.U49   333.7'2'02573   79-53313
ISBN 0-912102-45-4

CONTENTS

INTRODUCTION

There is growing concern over global trends in resource depletion and degradation of the environment. The widely-publicized GLOBAL 2000 REPORT TO THE PRESIDENT, issued in 1981, described what the world might be like by the end of the century if present trends continue:

> The world in 2000 will be more crowded, more polluted, less stable ecologically, and more vulnerable to disruption than the world we live in now. For hundreds of millions of the desparately poor, the outlook for food and other necessities of life will be no better. For many it will be worse.

GLOBAL 2000 made projections, not predictions. It called for "vigorous and determined new initiatives" to deal with global environmental deterioration of "alarming proportions."

A few months before GLOBAL 2000 was published, the WORLD CONSERVATION STRATEGY was issued by the International Union for Conservation of Nature and Natural Resources, the umbrella organization of the world conservation movement. It found that

> Living resources essential for human survival and sustainable development are increasingly being destroyed or depleted. At the same time human demand for those resources is growing fast...If current rates of land degradation continue, close to one third of the world's arable land will be destroyed in the next 20 years. Similarly, by the end of this century (at present rates of clearance) the remaining area of unlogged productive tropical forest will be halved.

The WORLD CONSERVATION STRATEGY, like GLOBAL 2000, wasn't written by doom-sayers. It set forth specific steps to be taken by national governments, international agencies, and non-governmental organizations to meet the problem.

American leadership is essential to meeting the problem of the global environment. As a June 1983 policy paper of the Global Tomorrow Coalition (see page 38) stated, efforts to alter the global environmental trends underway

> depend on the cooperation of all nations but cannot succeed without renewed commitment from the United States. As the most powerful economic force on earth and the political leader of the western world, the United States must play a prominent role.

This book describes the international environmental activities of over a hundred American organizations: governmental agencies, citizens' groups, university institutes, foundations, professional associations, and scientific societies and academies. It is limited to U.S. organizations, although we have also included a few binational organizations (e.g., the Canada-United States Environmental Council), and some international organizations that are based in the U.S. and have many American members.

Listings are limited to organizations that have a continuing interest in international environmental affairs, and have programs that include political action, policy studies, public education, or action-oriented scientific research. The activities of the main actors are described in some detail.

The problem of the global environment has many dimensions. Many U.S. organizations concerned more generally with international relations, development in the Third World, population, hunger, wildlife protection, international biological research, and other related topics have been omitted, even though they may have an interest in this field.

This book was inspired by a publication issued by the U.S. Environmental Protection Agency in 1977, INTERNATIONAL ENVIRONMENTAL ISSUES: A PRELIMINARY RESOURCE GUIDE. We found that the EPA guide left out a number of important U.S. organizations concerned with international environmental matters, and included some with purely domestic concerns. In gathering the information for this book, we sent letters or questionnaires to all of the groups listed in the EPA guide, as well as all U.S.-based member organizations of the International Union for Conservation of Nature and Natural Resources, and many other organizations. Most of the information given is excerpted or paraphrased from the material supplied by the groups listed.

The GLOBAL 2000 REPORT TO THE PRESIDENT was followed by another Carter Administration report, GLOBAL FUTURE: TIME TO ACT, which looked at what the U.S. Government could do to meet the issues put forth in GLOBAL 2000. Its authors concluded that "the U.S. Government currently lacks the capacity to anticipate and deal effectively to these global issues," and made specific suggestions for acting on them.

Former President Jimmy Carter, calling attention to GLOBAL 2000 and GLOBAL FUTURE in a June 1983 address to the Global Tomorrow Coalition, discussed his concerns about current U.S. Government attitudes on global environmental problems:

> The deliberate across-the-board abandonment of U.S. leadership on environmental, resource, and related global issues is of grave concern to us all...We must realize that without leadership within our own country, concerted action is unlikely...Every passing year of inaction exacerbates existing human suffering and makes it increasingly difficult to use our abilities and resources to prevent even more serious problems in the future.

I appreciate the assistance of Nancy Matsumoto in compiling the information for this book, and the help of the many organizations who responded to our survey.

THADDEUS C. TRZYNA

September 1983

U.S. GOVERNMENT AGENCIES

Agencies of the Congress

OFFICE OF TECHNOLOGY ASSESSMENT
600 Pennsylvania Avenue, S.E.
Washington, D.C. 20515
202-224-9241

The Office of Technology Assessment (OTA), an agency of the Congress, was formed in 1974 to help the Congress anticipate and plan for the consequences of the uses of technology. OTA "provides an independent and objective source of information about the impacts, both beneficial and adverse, of technological applications, and identifies policy alternatives for technology-related issues." The basic function of the Office is "to provide congressional committees with assessments or studies that identify the broad range of consequences, social as well as physical, which can be expected to accompany various policy choices affecting the use of technologies. More specifically, the functions of OTA are to identify existing or probable impacts of technology or technological programs and, where possible, ascertain cause-and-effect relationships; identify alternative programs for achieving requisite goals; make estimates and comparisons of the impacts of alternative methods and programs; present findings of completed analyses to the appropriate legislative authorities; identify areas where additional research or data collection is required to provide support for assessments; and undertake such additional associated activities as may be directed."

Many of OTA's studies deal with topics related to the future of the global environment, e.g., the energy potential of biomass, alternative energy futures, nuclear proliferation safeguards, the world food supply, the effects of nuclear war, and oil transportation by tankers. In 1982, the Office completed a study of "Global Models, World Futures, and Public Policy." Pub: Reports; annual report; informational brochures. Single-page summaries are issued for new reports.

Executive Office of the President

COUNCIL ON ENVIRONMENTAL QUALITY
722 Jackson Place, N.W.
Washington, D.C. 20006
202-395-5700

The Council on Environmental Quality (CEQ) is part of the Executive Office of the President and consists of three members appointed by the President, one of whom is designated by the President as Chairman. CEQ was set up by the National

Environmental Policy Act of 1969 (NEPA) to formulate and recommend national policies to promote the improvement of the quality of the environment. It develops and recommends to the President national policies which further environmental quality; performs a continuing analysis of changes or trends in the national environment; reviews and appraises programs of the federal government to determine their contributions to sound environmental policy; conducts studies, research, and analyses relating to ecological systems and environmental quality; and prepares an annual environmental quality report.

Under the Nixon, Ford, and Carter administrations, CEQ took an increasingly active role in trying to bring to bear U.S. Government resources on the problems of the world environment. The Council's chairmen during the Carter Administration, Charles Warren and later Gus Speth, initiated and led several important projects in the field, including the GLOBAL 2000 REPORT TO THE PRESIDENT and GLOBAL FUTURE (see the introduction to this book).

Under the Reagan Administration, an Interagency Global Issues Work Group was established in 1981 to develop "an overall Administration approach to international environmental issues." The Work Group was set up to "define and articulate policies as guidance for U.S. environmental activities both domestically and internationally. Other priorities...were to examine the possibility for improving the environmental forecasting ability within the Executive Branch and to develop an inventory of U.S. international environmental bilateral and multilateral agreements and other international obligations."

The "policy principles" for U.S. international environmental programs adopted by the Reagan Administration are as follows:

    -- "A healthy environment is fundamental to the well-being of mankind.

    -- "Economic growth and social progress are necessary conditions for effective implementation of policies which will protect the global environment and promote wise use of the earth's natural resource base.

    -- "Environmental policy should be based on the interests of present and future generations. The most successful policies are those which promote liberty and individual rights, as well as protection of the physical environment.

    -- "Nations should pursue economic development in furtherance of the security and well-being of their citizens in a manner which is sensitive to environmental concerns. Due respect should be given to different approaches which various nations may adopt to integrate environmental considerations into development strategies based on their particular national values and priorities.

    -- "Careful stewardship of the earth's natural resources can contribute significantly to sound economic development. Individual ownership of property, and free and well-developed markets in products and capital, are powerful incentives for resource conservation. These institutions best promote the use of renewable resources and the development of substitutes for nonrenewable resources, ensuring continued resource availability and environmental quality.

    -- "When environmental problems extend beyond the boundaries of any one nation, all affected nations should participate in investigating the nature of the problem, understanding its implications, and developing cost-effective responses.

-- "Governments, like individuals, should act so as to minimize environmental degradation. Decisions on environmental policies and programs should take into account the concerns of those closest to the problems and most directly affected.

-- "Increased scientific understanding of environmental problems, and improved methods of forecasting environmental conditions, are needed to address environmental issues in an effective and efficient manner. Ultimately, resolution of environmental problems which are global in nature will be determined by the quality and credibility of scientific and technical knowledge as well as by the degree of cooperation among nations, including the effective involvement of private sector institutions."

CEQ's recent involvement in international issues has included (1) meetings with Canadian officials on transboundary acid rain problems; (2) continuing to cooperate in international efforts on protection of the ozone layer, particularly within the structures of the United Nations Environment Programme (UNEP) and the Organization for Economic Co-operation and Development (OECD); (3) working within OECD on toxic chemicals issues; (4) efforts to deal with the transboundary movement of hazardous waste; and (5) involvement in a number of other U.S. Government activities relating to international environmental affairs, including marine pollution, tropical forests, arid regions, biological diversity, wildlife conservation, and protection of natural resources in the Caribbean.

Contact: A. Alan Hill, Chairman, CEQ. Pub: ENVIRONMENTAL QUALITY: ANNUAL REPORT OF THE COUNCIL ON ENVIRONMENTAL QUALITY.

Executive Departments

DEPARTMENT OF AGRICULTURE
U.S. FOREST SERVICE
P.O. Box 2417
Washington, D.C. 20013
202-447-5748

The Forest Service's International Forestry Staff assists the U.S. Agency for International Development (USAID) in locating and recruiting forestry specialists to identify, design, and implement forestry development projects in developing countries. It has also provided scientific and management support for USAID projects on production, conversion, and use of biomass for energy.

DEPARTMENT OF AGRICULTURE
U.S. FOREST SERVICE
INSTITUTE OF PACIFIC ISLANDS FORESTRY
1151 Punchbowl Street, Room 323
Honolulu, Hawaii 96813
808-546-5669

The Institute of Pacific Islands Forestry is part of the Forest Service's Pacific Southwest Forest and Range Experiment Station, headquartered in Berkeley, California. While much of the Institute's work focuses on Hawaii and other U.S. islands in the Pacific, projects are also done in cooperation with other governments in the Pacific region. Activities include making vegetation maps and forest surveys, research on traditional agroforestry, reforestation, and wildlife conservation. The Pacific Islands Forestry Information Center (PACIFIC) provides technical reference and bibliographic services to foresters and specialists in related fields in the western Pacific. Pub: Directory of experts in tropical forestry in the Asia-Pacific region.

DEPARTMENT OF AGRICULTURE
U.S. FOREST SERVICE
INSTITUTE OF TROPICAL FORESTRY
P.O. Box AQ
Rio Piedras, Puerto Rico 00928
809-763-3939

The Institute of Tropical Forestry (Instituto de Dasonomia Tropical, in Spanish) is part of the Forest Service's Southern Forest Experiment Station, headquartered in New Orleans. It has three main functions: (1) to serve as a source of information about tropical forests and forestry; (2) to generate new knowledge on this subject; and (3) to promote application of forestry knowledge in Puerto Rico and the U.S. Virgin Islands and, as prescribed by national policies, in other tropical areas. Much of the Institute's work in Puerto Rico and the Virgin Islands has application to other islands in the West Indies and to other tropical regions of the Americas. In addition, over 200 foreign students of tropical forestry have attended special three-month training courses. Research has been conducted in a number of other Caribbean and Latin American countries, and in cooperation with several international organizations. Recent major projects have focused on plantation culture, tropical forest wildlife, and protection of endangered species, and the role of tropical forests in the world carbon cycle. Pub: Annual Letter (report); research papers, research notes, technical reports.

DEPARTMENT OF COMMERCE
NATIONAL OCEANIC AND ATMOSPHERIC ADMINISTRATION
Washington, D.C. 20230
202-377-2985

Many of NOAA's functions have important international aspects. It conducts an integrated program of management, research, and services related to the protection and rational use of living marine resources; protects marine mammals; conducts research and development aimed at providing alternatives to ocean dumping, and developing sound national policies in the areas of ocean mining and energy; and acquires, stores, and disseminates worldwide environmental data through a system of meteorological, oceanographic, geodetic, and seismological data centers.

NOAA's National Marine Fisheries Service has an Office of International Fisheries Affairs (which includes Foreign Fisheries Analysis, International Organizations and Agreements, and International Fisheries Development and Services divisions), and an Office of Marine Mammals and Endangered Species.

NOAA's Office of Research and Development has a Programs and International Activities Office; and NOAA Office of Oceanic and Atmospheric Services has an International Affairs Office.

DEPARTMENT OF ENERGY
Washington, D.C. 20545
202-252-5000

The <u>Office of the Assistant Secretary for International Affairs</u> is responsible
for developing, managing, and directing Department of Energy programs related to
the international aspects of overall energy policy. The Office "ensures that
U.S. international energy policies and programs conform with national goals,
legislation, and treaty obligations, and assists the Secretary of Energy in
providing the President with independent technical advice on international
energy negotiations." In addition to assessing world price and supply trends
and supporting U.S. policies on international nuclear nonproliferation and the
international fuel cycle, it coordinates cooperative international energy
programs and maintains relationships with foreign governments and international
organizations. Most of the bilateral agreements in energy technologies which
the U.S. has signed relate to nuclear or fossil-fuel energy. However, there
have also been programs on geothermal sources with Iceland, Italy, and Mexico;
on radioactive waste management with West Germany and Sweden; and on a wide
range of energy areas, including solar and geothermal sources, with the USSR.

DEPARTMENT OF HEALTH AND HUMAN SERVICES
NATIONAL INSTITUTE OF ENVIRONMENTAL HEALTH SCIENCES (NIEHS)
P.O. Box 12233
Research Triangle Park, North Carolina 27709
919-541-2111

The general purpose of NIEHS is to support and conduct basic research focused on
the interaction between man and potentially toxic or harmful agents in his
environment. NIEHS is a Collaborating Center of the World Health Organization,
and supplies WHO with information, expertise, and consultation in the field of
environmental health. The Institute has also collaborated with Soviet
organizations on health problems associated with environmental pollution, under
the U.S.-USSR Medical Science and Public Health Cooperative Agreement, and the
joint Agreement on Cooperation in the Field of Environmental Protection. Under
the U.S.-Japan Cooperative Medical Sciences Program, NIEHS has worked with
Japanese institutions on problems of environmentally-induced cancer. The
Institute has been active in a number of other cooperative international
efforts, as well.

DEPARTMENT OF THE INTERIOR
Washington, D.C. 20240
202-343-6971

The <u>Office of the Assistant Secretary for Territorial and International Affairs</u>
is responsible for activities pertaining to U.S. territories and for the
coordination of the international affairs of the Department of the Interior. In
the international field, the Office "serves as the focal point for analysis,
development, and review of the Department's policy and programs pertaining to
international activities and the opportunities for support of U.S. foreign
policy through the use of the Department's natural resource and environmental
expertise."

DEPARTMENT OF THE INTERIOR
NATIONAL PARK SERVICE
Washington, D.C. 20240
202-523-5260

The U.S. National Park Service cooperates with other countries to assist in the development, management, and administration of national parks in two ways. First, the Service responds to requests from other countries for certain types of technical assistance. Such requests could be in the field of park planning, interpretation, environmental education, natural and cultural resource management, and other related fields. The assistance normally involves selecting and sending National Park Service personnel to the requesting countries for a specified period of time for consultancies, in-country training, professional work assignments, or joint research.

Second, the Service, on request, designs and provides U.S. training and study opportunities for professional park people from other countries. The duration of these training programs may vary from one day to one year. One such program is the month-long International Seminar on National Parks and Equivalent Reserves, held annually with the cosponsorship of the Canadian National Parks Service and the University of Michigan. Participants' costs are borne by their own governments or by other funding organizations.

The coordination and management of these activities is handled by the International Park Affairs Division of NPS. The National Park Service does not have funds to sponsor, host, or provide grants to foreign nationals, nor can the Service provide on-site technical assistance with its own funds. Such costs have been met with money from the foreign governments involved and international organizations such as the World Wildlife Fund, UNESCO, the World Bank, and the Food and Agriculture Organization of the UN. Also, U.S. Government agencies such as the Agency for International Development and the U.S. Information Agency have provided funds for the same purpose.

DEPARTMENT OF THE INTERIOR
UNITED STATES FISH AND WILDLIFE SERVICE
Washington, D.C. 20240
202-343-5188

The U.S. Fish and Wildlife Service has been formally involved in international wildlife matters since the passage of the Lacey Act in 1900. This legislation regulates trade and commerce in foreign "birds or animals" by making importation of illegally-taken wildlife an offense under U.S. law, thus assisting other nations in protecting their own wildlife resources.

The Lacey Act was the first instance in which Congress gave international conservation responsibility to the Fish and Wildlife Service. By 1916, the U.S. had signed a migratory bird treaty with Great Britain for Canada. Subsequently, similar migratory bird treaties were concluded with Mexico, Japan, and the USSR containing management, research, and habitat protection provisions.

Passage of the U.S. Endangered Species Act of 1973, "perhaps the broadest and most powerful single piece of conservation legislation in existence," gave the Fish and Wildlife Service the authority it needed to become a fully-effective international conservation force. As a result, in March 1976, the International

Affairs Staff was set up under the Service's Deputy Director, with responsibility to "bring focus, balance, and a systematic approach to Service-wide international activities."

In recent years, Fish and Wildlife Service international activities have focused on the following areas:

-- Excess Foreign Currency Program. In 1977, Fish and Wildlife, in cooperation with the National Park Service, initiated wildlife management programs in India, Pakistan, and Egypt using excess foreign currencies under Public Law 480. These funds, derived from the sale of surplus agricultural products, must be used in the countries of origin whenever available, and can fund activities which are deemed useful in the conservation of threatened or endangered species. Projects assist foreign governments in implementing their own conservation programs, with special emphasis on protecting species that are on the U.S. Endangered or Threatened Species lists. They include research, management, and education (including public awareness and professional training).

-- U.S.-Mexico Joint Cooperation. The U.S.-Mexico Joint Committee on Wildlife Conservation was established by the U.S. Fish and Wildlife Service and its Mexican counterpart agency, the Direccion General de la Fauna Silvestre, in 1975. Areas identified for joint work include endangered species, migratory bird management, law enforcement, wildlife research, and training. Projects under the joint committee are also carried out by the National Audubon Society and National Wildlife Federation, and New Mexico and Texas state agencies. Studies have been done on the California condor, Mexican wolf and grizzly bear, Sonoran pronged antelope, and birds of the Chiapan cloud forest, among other species.

-- U.S.-USSR Program. The U.S.-USSR Agreement on Cooperation in the Field of Environmental Protection, signed in 1972 and renewed in 1977 and 1982 for additional five-year periods, has dealt in large part with wildlife and ecosystems protection. The area of this agreement in which the Fish and Wildlife Service has been involved concerns "Protection of Nature and the Organization of Preserves." The Service's work with the USSR has included research on and captive breeding of threatened and endangered species, such as the black-footed ferret, the Siberian steppe polecat, and the musk ox, as well as ecosystem comparison studies of northern taiga and tundra, and migratory bird research on Siberian cranes, peregrine falcons, snow geese, and other waterfowl. Joint botanical research has also been conducted, emphasizing rare, threatened, and endangered species and the botanical relationships of U.S. and Soviet mountain areas. One of the major accomplishments of the joint program was the conclusion in 1978 of a bilateral Convention on the Conservation of Migratory Birds and their Environment, which provides for habitat preservation measures and protection for birds migrating between Siberia and North America.

-- Programs in Central and South America. Habitat destruction in the Western Hemisphere has resulted in problems for U.S. migratory species as well as for indigenous wildlife in Central and South America. Under the Carter Administration, the Service worked to revitalize the Convention on Nature Protection and Wildlife Preservation in the Western Hemisphere. That Convention calls for establishment of national parks, reserves, and monuments; protection of natural resources and of migratory and endangered birds; and regulation of trade and commerce in protected species of flora and fauna. The Service participated in a series of technical meetings sponsored by the Organization of

American States to gather information on Hemisphere conservation problems, suggest remedies, and make recommendations for reconvening the parties to the Convention leading to remedial actions. The Service has cooperated with various national governments and international agencies in Latin America in training of wildlife personnel and in conducting wildlife surveys.

-- U.S.-Japan Cooperative Program. In 1964, the Department of the Interior entered into a cooperative agreement with the government of Japan on environmental protection. The U.S.-Japan Cooperative Program on Nature and Natural Resources (UJNR) functions through a series of panels, each of which speaks to a particular scientific, technological, or environmental issue of mutual interest to the two countries. The Fish and Wildlife Service is represented on the UNJR Panel on Conservation, Recreation, and Parks. Other activities concerning Japan have included attempts to speed implementation of the 1972 U.S.-Japan Convention for the Protection of Migratory Birds in Danger of Extinction, and attempts to alleviate the danger to waterbirds caused by the Japanese fishing technique of gill-netting.

-- U.S.-Canadian Cooperation. Cooperation between the U.S. and Canada in conservation of living resources has a long history going as far back as the signing of the Convention for the Protection of Migratory Birds in 1916. "Service invovement with these issues has traditionally remained at a background level." In recent years, however, "the Service has sought to elevate its involvement in these issues and to influence U.S. foreign policies in ways advantageous to Service conservation interests." Much of the cooperative work done with Canada is under the auspices of the International Joint Commission. The Fish and Wildlife Service participates in IJC sub-commissions organized by water basins that concern themselves with various boundary water problems.

-- Cooperative Program with Spain. Under a 1974 Treaty for Friendship and Cooperation, the U.S. and Spain have negotiated a Memorandum of Cooperation on Conservation of Natural and Cultural Resources. Funding for cooperative projects comes from payments made to Spain as compensation for placement of U.S. military bases in Spain. The Fish and Wildlife Service has been involved in several projects, including an assessment of problems in the Coto Donana ecosystem in Spain, the major wetland for migratory waterfowl in Western Europe.

-- CITES. The Convention on International Trade in Endangered Species of Wild Flora and Fauna, negotiated in Washington in 1973, controls international trade and commerce in certain species of endangered wildlife and plants. This convention represents a major international effort to protect threatened and endangered species by reducing the facility for moving such species and their parts from international trade. Within the Fish and Wildlife Service, separate organizations are responsible for the management and scientific aspects of CITES implementation in the U.S. Government: the Office of Endangered Species, and the Endangered Species Scientific Authority.

DEPARTMENT OF STATE
Washington, D.C. 20250
202-632-1554

The Bureau of Oceans and International Environmental and Scientific Affairs (OES) has principal responsibility within the Department of State for the formulation and implementation of policies and proposals for the scientific and technical aspects of U.S. relations with other countries and international organizations. It also has the management responsibility for a broad range of foreign policy issues and significant global problems related to oceans, fisheries, environment, population, nuclear technology, new energy technology, space, and other fields of advanced technology, and for cooperative efforts dealing with the application and transfer of technology. The Bureau advises the Secretary of State where scientific and technical factors or the Bureau's functional responsibilities are concerned; represents the Department in international negotiations in its area of responsibility; provides policy guidance to the U.S. oceanic, environmental, scientific and technological communities on activities and programs affecting foreign policy issues; assures effective coordination of policy responsibilities between the State Department and the U.S. Agency for International Development (USAID) in the field of science and technology; and directs a program under which scientific and technological and fisheries attaches are assigned to U.S. embassies.

The Bureau develops and directs the carrying out of policy recommendations relative to U.S. participation in international science and technology programs; in bilateral cooperative programs related to its area of interests; and in the activities of the international fisheries commissions of which the U.S. is a member. The OES Bureau is divided into the Office of Ocean Affairs, the Office of Fisheries Affairs, the Office of Environment and Health, the Office of Nuclear Energy and Energy Technology Affairs, the Office of Science and Technology, and the Office of the Coordinator of Population Affairs.

DEPARTMENT OF STATE
AGENCY FOR INTERNATIONAL DEVELOPMENT
Washington, D.C. 20523
202-632-1850

The Agency for International Development (AID or USAID) is responsible for conducting the U.S. foreign economic assistance program. It is currently carrying on activities in some 70 developing countries to "develop their human and economic resources, increase productive capacities, and improve the quality of human life as well as to promote economic or political stability in friendly countries."

USAID focuses its development assistance programs on "critical problem areas that affect the majority of the people in the developing countries." Its "functional sectors" or areas of concentration are (1) Agriculture, Rural Development, and Nutrition; (2) Health; (3) Population Planning; (4) Education and Human Resource Development; and (5) "Selected Development Activities," which deals with "a wide range of development concerns which do not fall within" the other four sectors, including energy and rapid urbanization. There is also a special regional program for the development of the Sahelian region of West Africa, carried out in cooperation with the governments of the Sahelian countries, other donor nations, and various multilateral organizations.

In the early 1970s, concern over the environmental and natural resource problems of developing countries, and USAID's role in dealing with them, arose both within the Agency and in non-governmental environmental and development organizations. In 1977, Congress gave USAID its first direct mandate in this area by adding "Environment and Natural Resources" to the list of development problems on which the Agency is directed to focus its efforts; authorized assistance for environmental and natural resource protection and management; and called upon the Agency to make special efforts to maintain and restore the natural resources of developing countries. In the years since, additional requirements and authority have been given to USAID to ensure the environmental soundness of the projects it supports and that it will be responsive to the environmental and natural resource needs of the assisted countries.

A 1980 study prepared for USAID by the Natural Resources Defense Council (AIDING THE ENVIRONMENT: A STUDY OF THE ENVIRONMENTAL POLICIES, PROCEDURES, AND PERFORMANCE OF THE U.S. AGENCY FOR INTERNATIONAL DEVELOPMENT, by Robert O. Blake and others) concluded that "within the last decade, [USAID] has changed from an agency which paid little conscious attention to environmental aspects of development into a leader within the international development assistance community in addressing the serious environmental problems confronting developing countries. AID is moving toward a program of assistance which is sensitive to the relationship between environment and development, and responsive to the needs of developing nations for assistance in protecting and managing critical natural resources."

USAID has an Environmental Affairs Coordinator in its Bureau for Program and Policy Coordination. The Agency's Bureau for Science and Technology includes a Directorate for Energy and Natural Resources, which in turn has an Office of Energy and an Office of Forestry, Environment, and Natural Resources. Each of USAID's four regional bureaus (Africa; Asia; Near East; and Latin America and the Caribbean) has staff assigned to coordinate environmental protection and natural resource management activities within its region.

In fiscal year 1983, nearly $120 million was committed to environmental and natural resource projects. Much of USAID's program is conducted through its overseas missions and offices; individual projects are carried out largely by contractors and consultants, and by U.S. "private voluntary organizations" (PVOs). The Country Development Strategy Statement (CDSS) that the Agency prepares for each USAID-supported country includes "a thorough compilation of environmental and natural resource data."

A few examples of current and recent USAID activities in environmental protection and natural resource management:

-- Funding to governments of certain developing countries and the International Union for Conservation of Nature and Natural Resources (IUCN) to produce a series of national conservation strategies patterned after IUCN's WORLD CONSERVATION STRATEGY.

-- The Environmental Training and Management in Africa (ETMA) project; see the entries for Clark University and the University of North Carolina.

-- Designing a program on coastal zone management for developing countries.

-- A regional program to develop energy planning capabilities in the countries of the Caribbean, including energy conservation and alternative energy technologies.

Pub: Reports, for example, ENVIRONMENTAL AND NATURAL RESOURCE MANAGEMENT IN DEVELOPING COUNTRIES: A REPORT TO CONGRESS (1979); FORESTRY RESOURCES DEVELOPMENT ASSISTANCE: A SELECTIVE BIBLIOGRAPHY OF REPORTS (1980); ENERGY ASSISTANCE POLICY PAPER (1981).

DEPARTMENT OF THE TREASURY
UNITED STATES CUSTOMS SERVICE
1301 Constitution Avenue, N.W.
Washington, D.C. 20229
202-566-5104

The U.S. Customs Service is responsible for enforcement of the U.S. laws
regarding importation and exportation of endangered species.

Independent Agencies

ENDANGERED SPECIES COMMITTEE
Room 4160, Department of the Interior Building
Washington, D.C. 20240
202-235-2771

Under the Endangered Species Act of 1973, federal agencies are required to
ensure that their actions are not likely to jeopardize the continued existence
of any endangered or threatened species, or result in the destruction or adverse
modification of critical habitats. This requirement extends to the protection
of migratory species and species outside the U.S., if covered by an
international treaty obligation of the U.S. The Endangered Species Committee
may grant exemptions to these requirements, however. The committee is composed
of the Secretary of the Interior, who is the chairman; the Secretary of
Agriculture, the Secretary of the Army, the Chairman of the Council of Economic
Advisors, the Administrator of the National Oceanic and Atmospheric
Administration, and "a person from each affected State, or if no State is
affected an otherwise qualified individual, appointed by the President for each
exemption application." Applications for exemptions are referred to Endangered
Species Review Boards, which make recommendations to the Endangered Species
Committee.

ENVIRONMENTAL PROTECTION AGENCY
Washington, D.C. 20460
202-382-2090

EPA's general mission is "to control and abate pollution in the areas of air,
water, solid waste, noise, radiation, and toxic substances" through "an
integrated, coordinated attack on environmental pollution in cooperation with
state and local governments." The goals of EPA's international work were
spelled out in the National Environmental Policy Act of 1969, which specifies
that "to the fullest extent possible, all agencies of the Federal Government
recognize the worldwide and long-range character of environmental problems and,
where consistent with the foreign policy of the United States, lend appropriate
support to initiatives, resolutions, and programs designd to maximize
international cooperation in anticipating and preventing a decline in the
quality of mankind's world environment."

The focal point of EPA's international work is the Office of International
Activities. It plans and coordinates EPA participation in programs of
multilateral international organizations to solve common environmental problems;
develops and directs EPA's bilateral exchanges with other countries of
technology and information; and serves as the liaison between the Department of

State and EPA on all international EPA programs and policies to ensure proper coordination with U.S. foreign policy goals. The Office has three major sections: the Western Hemisphere; Bilaterals; and Oceans and Regulatory divisions.

Currently, the major international problems of concern to EPA are (1) acid rain issues between the U.S. and Canada; (2) ocean dumping of wastes, including nuclear wastes; (3) regulation of chemicals, particularly in cooperation with the Organization for Economic Co-operation and Development (OECD); (4) exports of hazardous waste from the U.S.; (5) exports of unregistered pesticides from the U.S. and the potential for their subsequent re-importation as residues on foods; (6) the export of toxic substances and notification to the governments of importing countries; (7) depletion of stratospheric ozone by fluorocarbons and other man-made pollutants; (8) atmospheric carbon dioxide; and (9) mineral resource issues in Antarctica.

The multilateral organizations with which EPA is involved are the United Nations Environment Programme (UNEP); the Organization for Economic Co-operation and Development (OECD); the World Health Organization (WHO); the UN Economic Commission for Europe (ECE); the World Meteorological Organization (WMO); and the NATO Committee on the Challenges of Modern Society (CCMS).

Bilateral activities in which EPA is involved include cooperation with Canada on water quality, water resources, and air quality; cooperation with Mexico on border area water sanitation problems; joint research with West Germany under a 1974 agreement on environmental cooperation; exchange of information and cooperative research with the Netherlands; and a series of 14 research projects with Japan under a 1975 environmental agreement.

EPA has primary responsibility for the U.S. side of the U.S.-USSR agreement on cooperation in the field of environmental protection, which was signed in 1972 and extended for additional five-year terms in 1977 and 1982. The agreement calls for cooperative activity in 42 specific projects organized into 11 general areas: air pollution, water pollution, agricultural pollution, urban environment, nature conservation, marine pollution, biological/genetic effects, climatic effects, earthquake prediction, arctic/subarctic ecosystems, and legal/administrative measures. Since the Soviet invasion of Afghanistan, activities under the agreement have been at a low level, and no meetings of the joint committee have been held since 1979. However, a joint symposium on acid rain research is planned for 1984.

EPA is also responsible for the U.S. side of cooperative activities with the People's Republic of China, under an environmental protection protocol signed in 1980. So far, projects have focused on technical and health aspects of air pollution.

EPA's Scientific Activities Overseas program includes cooperative studies with India, Pakistan, Egypt, and Yugoslavia under general bilateral science and technology agreements with those countries.

The Office of International Activities conducts a foreign visitors program designed to introduce government officials, scientists, journalists, industrialists, and community leaders to the policies and programs of EPA and to initiate lasting relationships between EPA personnel and their counterparts abroad.

MARINE MAMMAL COMMISSION
1625 I Street, N.W.
Washington, D.C. 20006
202-653-6237

Established to ensure that the objectives of the Marine Mammal Protection Act of 1972 are achieved. The Act sets forth a national policy to prevent marine mammal species (whales, dolphins, porpoises, seals, sea lions, sea otters, etc.) and population stocks from diminishing, as a result of human activities, beyond which they cease to be a significant functioning element in the marine ecosystem. To this end, the Commission periodically reviews the status of marine mammal populations; manages a research program concerned with their conservation; and develops, reviews, and makes recommendations on U.S. Government activities and policies that affect their protection and conservation. Consults with a Committee of Scientific Advisors on Marine Mammals.

NATIONAL RESEARCH COUNCIL

A non-governmental organization. See entry on page 47.

NUCLEAR REGULATORY COMMISSION
1717 H Street, N.W.
Washington, D.C. 20555
301-492-7000

The general purposes of the NRC are to license and regulate the uses of nuclear energy in the United States to protect the public health and safety and the environment. NRC's Office of International Programs plans, develops, and implements programs of international cooperation, and formulates and recommends policies concerning nuclear exports and imports, international safeguards, and nonproliferation matters. The NRC has entered into nuclear regulatory information exchanges and cooperation arrangements with a number of countries. It also has bilateral research programs and cooperates closely with such multilateral agencies as the International Atomic Energy Agency (IAEA), European Atomic Energy Community (EURATOM), and the Nuclear Energy Agency of the Organisation for Economic Co-operation and Development (OECD).

PEACE CORPS
806 Connecticut Avenue, N.W.
Washington, D.C. 20526
202-254-5010

The Peace Corps, established in 1961 at the initiative of President John F. Kennedy, recruits and sends volunteers to Third-World countries to aid in their economic and social development. Currently, some 5,000 Peace Corps volunteers serve in 62 countries. They work primarily in the areas of agriculture and rural development, health, and education. Natural resource management and environmental protection are important elements of the program. Pub: Some 20 manuals have been issued in the "Appropriate Technologies for Development" series; these include, for example, TEACHING CONSERVATION IN DEVELOPING NATIONS (1977); RESOURCES FOR DEVELOPMENT (1981); and REFORESTATION IN ARID LANDS (1977). Other publications include FORESTRY CASE STUDIES (1981), and GLOSSARY OF ENVIRONMENTAL TERMS: SPANISH/ENGLISH, ENGLISH/SPANISH (1976).

SMITHSONIAN INSTITUTION
1000 Jefferson Drive, S.W.
Washington, D.C. 20520
202-357-1300

The Smithsonian Institution, a "trust instrumentality of the United States," was created in 1846 "for the increase and diffusion of knowledge among men." It consists of a complex structure of museums, centers, laboratories, institutes, offices, and other organizations. Several Smithsonian units are actively involved in international environmental matters; they include:

-- Office of International Affairs (202-357-2627). Fosters and coordinates international aspects of Smithsonian research and cultural exchange programs. A particular responsibility is the development of opportunties for scholarly cooperation between the Smithsonian and foreign institutions. The Office also administers a program of short-term visits by foreign officials and scholars.

-- Office of Biological Conservation. Established in 1978, this is part of the Office of the Assistant Secretary for Science. It seeks to "develop an awareness in the mind of our [Smithsonian] colleagues and the general public to the ever-present changes in the environment caused by human activity and thus serves as a minitoring and warning system. This we have been accomplishing by providing expertise based on the research data of the scientists in various bureaux [of the Smithsonian] to help government and non-governmental agencies, and by many publications in the popular press about natural resource conservation...We often see our labor result in concrete, positive decisions on the part of the U.S. Government." The Office represents the Smithsonian in various U.S. Government and international forums on world conservation issues. Particular concerns are deforestation of tropical areas and the worldwide commerce in endangered animal and plant species.

-- National Zoological Park (Rock Creek Park, Washington, D.C. 20009, 202-357-1300). Includes programs of research on and conservation of endangered species, both at the National Zoo in Rock Creek Park and at its Conservation and Research Center (CRC) near Front Royal, Virginia. Conservation-oriented research work is also done abroad, e.g., on tigers in Nepal; the giant civit of Sulawesi, Indonesia; and the red howler monkey in Venezuela.

-- Smithsonian Tropical Research Institute (mailing address: APO Miami, Florida 34002), located on Barro Colorado Island in Panama. STRI is a major center for advanced studies in tropical biology. Also administers a tropical forest reserve "which is less disturbed and has a more complete animal commmunity than any other equally accessible tract of tropical forest." STRI staff work on conservation-oriented research in various tropical regions throughout the world.

Pub: General periodicals are SMITHSONIAN magazine, a popular monthly; and SMITHSONIAN INSTITUTION RESEARCH REPORTS, issued 3 times a year by the Office of Public Affairs, which contains news of current research projects. SMITHSONIAN YEAR, a detailed annual report, lists the many other publications issued by units of the Smithsonian, including books, reports, papers, and periodicals.

U.S. NATIONAL COMMITTEE FOR MAN AND THE BIOSPHERE
Department of State (IO/UCS)
Washington, D.C. 20520
202-632-2762

A committee of the U.S. National Commission for UNESCO, the United Nations Educational, Scientific, and Cultural Organization. The U.S. National Committee for Man and the Biosphere is the U.S. component of UNESCO's worldwide Man and the Biosphere Program (MAB).

The objective of MAB is to "develop the basis within the natural and social sciences for the rational use and conservation of the biosphere - that portion of the earth's crust and lower atmosphere which contains life - and for the improvement of the global relationship between man and the environment. The aim, therefore, is to produce research results which will provide improved management strategies for decision makers and resource managers. To achieve the goal, policy and decision makers participate in the setting of research directions and provide continuing guidance until the goals are reached."

In each of some 80 countries now participating, a national committee defines and organizes research activities on particular national problems designed to respond to the international framework. In the U.S., under the auspices of the National Committee, cooperative work is done in 14 areas: tropical forests; temperate forests; grazing lands; arid zones; fresh water; mountains; islands; biosphere reserves; pesticides/fertilizer; engineering works; urban ecosystems; demographic change; perception of environmental quality; and pollution.

NON-GOVERNMENTAL ORGANIZATIONS

AMERICAN ASSOCIATION FOR THE ADVANCEMENT OF SCIENCE (AAAS)
1515 Massachusetts Avenue, N.W.
Washington, D.C. 20005
202-467-4400

The "world's largest federation of scientific and engineering societies," AAAS counts some 280 affiliated organizations as institutional members; there are also some 135,000 individual members. Objectives include furthering the work of scientists and facilitating cooperation among them, and improving the effectiveness of science in promoting human welfare.

The AAAS Office of International Science (OIS) administers a range of programs and activities related to international science and engineering, including bilateral and multilateral cooperative projects and exchanges. "In all of its programs, OIS aims to further understanding of global problems that have substantial scientific and technological components, and to provide the best information possible from the scientific community to decisionmakers at national and international levels."

Current and recent OIS projects include:

-- Climate Project: "Environmental and Societal Consequences of a Possible CO_2-Induced Climate Change." Brings together experts from the physical, biological, and social sciences with public policy experts to consider the impacts of a change in the global climatic regime, caused by an increase in atmospheric carbon dioxide. Directed by the AAAS Committee on Climate.

-- Arid Lands. The AAAS Committee on Arid Lands and OIS work together in coordinating activities designed to promote public understanding of arid lands problems and communication among scientists engaged in arid lands research.

-- Global Seminar on the Role of Scientific and Engineering Societies in Development. This was held in New Delhi, India, in December 1980, in cooperation with Indian scientific bodies, to discuss the unique characteristics of the scientific and engineering societies and how they can help problems of development in the Third World.

-- Methods for Environmental Studies. A review and evaluation of existing methodologies for conducting natural resource surveys and environmental baseline studies in developing countries.

-- Western Hemisphere Cooperation Project. AAAS was a founding member and provides the secretariat for the Interciencia Association, a federation of scientific associations in the Western Hemisphere, with the aim of promoting cooperative uses of science and technology to benefit the peoples of the Americas. The federation publishes a trilingual journal, INTERCIENCIA (bimonthly), which focuses on science and technology for development; and sponsors international symposia on many topics, including environmental issues.

Other AAAS international activities include symposia on international scientific and engineering issues at the Association's annual meeting; the AAAS Consortium of Affiliates for International Programs, which brings together AAAS affiliated organizations with an interest in the international aspects of their disciplines; sponsoring Science, Engineering and Diplomacy Fellows in the Department of State; and advising U.S. Government agencies.

Pub: SCIENCE, weekly, with frequent coverage of international environmental topics. SCIENCE 83, ten times a year. CONSORTIUM NOTES, three times a year (Consortium of Affiliates for International Programs). Symposium series, published for AAAS by Westview Press. Numerous books and reports, e.g., HANDBOOK ON DESERTIFICATION INDICATORS (1978); CLIMATE CHANGE: A RESEARCH AGENDA (1980-81). Audiotapes.

AMERICAN ASSOCIATION OF ZOOLOGICAL PARKS AND AQUARIUMS (AAZPA)
INTERNATIONAL SPECIES INVENTORY SYSTEM (ISIS)
Minnesota Zoological Garden
12101 Johnny Cake Ridge Road
Apple Valley, Minnesota 55124
612-432-9010

The International Species Inventory System (ISIS), a program of the AAZPA, is a computer-based information system for animals in captivity. It now includes over 50,000 living mammals and birds, plus tens of thousands of their ancestors, from about 150 institutions in North America and Europe. "The spectacular loss of natural habitat in the natural world means that many captive populations must become self-sustaining, rather then dependent on wild-caught stock. To achieve this goal, it is necessary to have good biological data on all individuals available to everyone... Over the long term, captive populations of many species may be all that we have left. For such species, future existence will depend on careful cooperative management of the population's genetics and demography. This requires good biological information, as far back in time as possible. ISIS is a cost-effective method of assembling this information." Contact: Nathan Flesness, Project Director. Pub: ISIS SPECIES DISTRIBUTION REPORT, semiannual (over 3,000 pages, for participating organizations).

AMERICAN CETACEAN SOCIETY (ACS)
P.O. Box 4416
San Pedro, California 90731
213-548-6279

"Founded in 1967 to gather information on and aid in the protection of marine mammals, with special focus on cetacea, which is the scientific name for the order that includes whales, dolphins, and porpoises." Concerns include supporting international efforts to protect these species. 2,000 members. Contact: Karla Slap, Executive Director. Pub: WHALEWATCHER: JOURNAL OF THE AMERICAN CETACEAN SOCIETY, quarterly. WHALE NEWS: NEWSLETTER OF THE AMERICAN CETACEAN SOCIETY, monthly.

AMERICAN COMMITTEE FOR INTERNATIONAL CONSERVATION, INC. (ACIC)
c/o Barbara Bramble, Secretary
National Wildlife Federation
1412 16th Street, N.W.
Washington, D.C. 20036
202-797-6896

Association of U.S. nongovernmental organizations concerned with international
conservation. Works to stimulate and coordinate members' international
activities. In the past few years, ACIC has been functioning increasingly as a
national committee of the International Union for Conservation of Nature and
Natural Resources (IUCN; see separate entry). Holds meetings about six times a
year, usually in Washington, D.C. Contact: Patricia J. Scharlin, Chairman, c/o
Sierra Club International Earthcare Center, 228 E. 45th Street, New York, New
York 10017, 212-867-0080.

AMERICAN PETROLEUM INSTITUTE (API)
2101 L Street, N.W.
Washington, D.C. 20037
202-457-7000

API's Environmental Affairs Department cooperates with domestic and
international agencies in sponsoring environmental research studies, surveys,
data gathering projects, and information exchanges aimed at furthering the
goals of protecting and improving the environment. In 1981, the Department
budgeted over $4 million for its environmental research program. It
participates in such activities as the United Nations Environment Programme
Seminar on Petroleum Industry Operations, and the biennial Oil Spill Conference,
which is co-sponsors with the U.S. Environmental Protection Agency and the U.S.
Coast Guard. Contact: George T. Patton, Director, Environmental Affairs.

Representative recent projects: Contingency Planning for Hazardous Spills;
Ozone-Hydrocarbon Control Strategy; Environmental Expenditure Survey (of the
petroleum industry); Use of Economic Incentives for Environmental Protection.
Pub: AIR AND WATER CONSERVATION ABSTRACTS, weekly. Research reports.
ENVIRONMENTAL RESEARCH: ANNUAL STATUS REPORT.

AMERICAN PLANNING ASSOCIATION (APA)
1776 Massachusetts Avenue, N.W.
Washington, D.C. 20036
202-872-0611

Formed by the consolidation of the former American Institute of Planners (AIP)
and American Society of Planning Officials (ASPO). Members are professional
city and regional planners, public officials, academics, and others interested
in planning. APA recently formed an International Planning Division. Pub: APA
JOURNAL, quarterly. PLANNING, monthly. APA NEWS, monthly.

AFRICAN WILDLIFE FOUNDATION
1717 Massachusetts Avenue, N.W.
Washington, D.C. 20036
202-265-8394

Organized in 1961 as the African Wildlife Leadership Foundation. "From the beginning our premise has been that in the final analysis only the African peoples themselves can save their fabulous wildlife heritage." Supports training centers for African wildlife managers in Tanzania and Cameroon. Sponsors conservation education programs in many African countries, including the widely-publicized Wildlife Clubs of Kenya. Provides technical and financial assistance for anti-poaching efforts, and headed up a consortium of the world's major conservation groups to protect mountain gorillas in Rwanda. Conducts and supports research efforts, including the Serengeti Ecological Monitoring Program in Tanzania, and projects for domestication of wildlife in several countries. Nairobi Office: P.O. Box 48177, Nairobi, Kenya. Contact: Robert P. Smith, President. Pub: WILDLIFE NEWS, quarterly.

ANIMAL WELFARE INSTITUTE
P.O. Box 3650
Washington, D.C. 20007
202-337-2333

Founded in 1951 to promote the humane treatment of animals. "While the Institute is interested in every phase of animal welfare, a major concern is humane safeguards in the use of animals for research and medicine." Other aims include preservation of species threatened by extinction. International concerns focus on commercial whaling and the international traffic in wild animals and animal products. Awards Albert Schweitzer Medal annually for outstanding contributions to animal welfare. Contact: Christine Stevens, President. Pub: INFORMATION REPORT, quarterly newsletter. Books and manuals, e.g., THE BIRD BUSINESS (1981); WHALES VERSUS WHALERS (1981); ENDANGERED SPECIES HANDBOOK. Educational materials.

ARIZONA-SONORA DESERT MUSEUM
Route 9, Box 900
Tucson, Arizona 85704
602-883-1380

In addition to operating a museum, conducts research related to the conservation of the natural resources of the Sonoran Desert region of northern Mexico and the southwestern U.S. Recent work has included studies of the ecology of the Gulf of California, the marine turtles of the Pacific Coast of Mexico, agroecosystems, and desert plants with underexploited economic value. Contact: Dan Davis, Director. Pub: SONORENSIS, quarterly. THE SONORAN DESERT (book, 1980). Papers and articles in publications of other organizations.

ASPEN INSTITUTE FOR HUMANISTIC STUDIES
717 Fifth Avenue
New York, New York 10022
212-759-1053

The Aspen Institute, an international, nonprofit organization, brings together
leading citizens from all sectors of society throughout the world to consider
issues of modern times. It seeks to identify and evaluate alternative
approaches to major current problems while considering the relationship among
issues and the need for cooperative effort among nations. "The Institute's
most precious asset is its recognition as a neutral forum for bringing together
diverse persons of high quality." International environmental and resource
issues have been dealt with under two of the Institute's long-term programs,
International Affairs; and Science, Technology and Humanism. Examples of
individual activities include meetings on nuclear waste management, world
hunger, climate change, and energy. Pub: ASPEN INSTITUTE CHRONICLE,
newsletter. Books, e.g., ENERGY FUTURES OF DEVELOPING COUNTRIES (1980); THE
CLIMATE MANDATE (1979). Monographs; speeches, reports, and reprints; seminar
readings; annual report. Catalog available.

ASSOCIATION FOR ARID LANDS STUDIES (AALS)
c/o International Center for Arid and Semi-Arid Land Studies
Texas Tech University
P.O. Box 4620
Lubbock, Texas 79409

Founded in 1977, and with 164 members, AALS is an organization of social
scientists and humanists which works "to encourage an increased general
awareness of the problems and potentials of the arid and semi-arid lands of the
world and of man's adjustment to and impact upon them." Holds an annual meeting
and organizes symposia and other professional sessions. 1981 annual meeting
included sessions on physical phenomena in arid lands; water resources;
legislation and law; urban planning and development; human response to the arid
environment; economic activity; and historical perspectives. Contact: Idris R.
Traylor, Jr., Executive Director. Pub: AALS NEWS, semiannual newsletter.
Abstracts of papers given at the annual meeting.

BUREAU OF NATIONAL AFFAIRS, INC. (BNA)
1231 25th Street, N.W.
Washington, D.C. 20037
202-452-4428

BNA is a commercial firm that publishes newsletters and looseleaf information
services designed for a business and legal audience. Among its many
publications is INTERNATIONAL ENVIRONMENT REPORTER, monthly, which gives
detailed current information on political and legal aspects of environmental
regulation, focusing mainly on what is happening in industrialized countries and
in international organizations. The service also includes a 3-binder reference
file of treaties and other international agreements and texts of key European
environmental regulations, which are updated as necessary.

CALIFORNIA INSTITUTE OF PUBLIC AFFAIRS (CIPA)
P.O. Box 10
Claremont, California 91711
714-624-5212

CIPA, founded in 1969 and affiliated with The Claremont Colleges, is an
independent foundation for research, publishing, and public service. Its main
purpose is to work for better communication of facts, ideas, and opinion about
the character, problems, and future development of California. A special
interest is environmental and natural resource policy. This has led to
international projects that try to draw on the experiences of other countries
to improve the way things are done in California, and to bring to
bear California's substantial experience in environmental management on the
problems of developing countries. For example, under a grant from the German
Marshall Fund of the U.S., three French experts in agricultural land use visited
California in spring 1983 to discuss whether France's pioneering program of
agricultural land preservation has any relevance to California's situation; and
CIPA is planning a series of intensive workshops on the role of conservation in
development for selected Third-World students at major California universities.

CIPA has also edited and published information guides on international
environmental topics, including the WORLD DIRECTORY OF ENVIRONMENTAL
ORGANIZATIONS (with the Sierra Club, second edition, 1976); THE UNITED STATES
AND THE GLOBAL ENVIRONMENT: A GUIDE TO AMERICAN ORGANIZATIONS CONCERNED WITH
INTERNATIONAL ENVIRONMENTAL ISSUES (1983); and THE NUCLEAR POWER ISSUE: A GUIDE
TO WHO'S DOING WHAT IN THE U.S. AND ABROAD (1981). Similar books have been
issued on world food and population problems. Contact: Thaddeus C. (Ted)
Trzyna, President.

CANADA-UNITED STATES ENVIRONMENTAL COUNCIL (CUSEC)
c/o James G. Deane, American Co-Chairman
Defenders of Wildlife
1244 19th Street, N.W.
Washington, D.C. 20036
202-659-9510

Formed in 1974 by major U.S. and Canadian conservation and environmental groups
to facilitate interchange of information and cooperative action on questions of
concern to the two countries. Issues of concern in recent years have included
acid rain, Great Lakes water quality, the Arctic International Wildlife Refuge
and its caribou herd, whale protection, oil drilling in the Beaufort Sea, and
international river systems. Contact: James G. Deane, American Co-Chairman.

CENTER FOR ACTION ON ENDANGERED SPECIES, INC. (CAES)
175 W. Main Street
Ayer, Massachusetts 01432
617-772-0445

Formed in 1973 as Endangered Species Productions; changed its name in 1978.
Researches and produces educational materials and public information on
threatened wildlife. Sponsors the country-jazz band Condor, which presents
"environmental pop music with a multi-media light show." Sponsors
"locally-executed wall murals on conservation themes" in developing countries.
Operates the Jojoba Project to promote cultivation of the jojoba plant as a

substitute for sperm whale oil. Advocacy on national and international levels.
Works with groups in various developing countries, including those in the Indian
Ocean region. Contact: Phoebe Wray, Executive Director. Pub: NEWSLETTER,
occasional. Books and monographs, e.g., THE SPERM WHALE (1979). Teaching
tools; slides; posters; records.

CENTER FOR ENVIRONMENTAL EDUCATION, INC.
625 Ninth Street, N.W.
Washington, D.C. 20001
202-737-6300

Established in 1972 "to inform people about environmental isssues and encourage
citizen involvement in improving environmental quality." Primary attention is
given to marine issues, particularly the survival of whales, seals, and sea
turtles worldwide. U.S. Government policies have been a special concern.
Supports research. Contact: Thomas B. Grooms, Executive Director. Pub:
ENVIRONMENTAL EDUCATION REPORT, ten times a year. THE WHALE REPORT, quarterly
newsletter. THE SEAL REPORT, newsletter. THE SEA TURTLE REPORT, newsletter.
Educational materials.

CENTER FOR LAW AND SOCIAL POLICY (CLASP)
1751 N Street, N.W.
Washington, D.C. 20036
202-872-0670

The Center is a foundation-funded public-interest law firm that specializes in
representing nonprofit public groups with respect to significant issues in
economic, environmental, human rights, and social areas. In the field of
international relations, CLASP "is dedicated to representing previously
unrepresented segments of the public with respect to significant foreign affairs
decision-making." Among its primary objectives are (1) to reform the process of
formulating U.S. positions on international issues by having foreign affairs
agencies follow open procedures, and the interested public institutionally
included in such processes, and (2) to represent U.S. and international public
groups in the decision-making of U.S. and intergovernmental agencies.

In recent years, CLASP activities in the international environmental field have
focused on marine issues, particularly oil tanker safety, ocean dumping, and the
international Law of the Sea.

    -- Oil Tanker Safety. Since 1973, CLASP has represented national
environmental organizations in efforts to achieve environmentally-sound
construction, operational, and personnel standards for oil tankers. This has
involved, among other things, acting as advisors to several U.S. delegations
negotiating international treaties.

    -- Ocean Dumping. A CLASP attorney has been a member of a U.S.
Environmental Protection Agency-Department of State Advisory Committee on Ocean
Dumping since 1978. Center attorneys have also represented several
environmental groups at international meetings on the London Dumping Convention.
The Center has also been monitoring the activities of the International Atomic
Energy Agency and the Nuclear Energy Agency of the Organization for Economic
Co-operation and Development (OECD) in relation to ocean dumping of low-level
radioactive wastes.

-- The Law of the Sea. A CLASP attorney has been a member of the Secretary of State's advisory committee on the Law of the Sea, representing environmental organizations and participating in that committee's deliberations about U.S. participation in the Law of the Sea conferences. The Center's efforts have been focused on obtaining environmentally sound amendments to the articles dealing with whales, deepsea mining, scientific research, and vessel source pollution.

Contact: Clifton E. Curtis, attorney (international marine environment issues). Pub: Papers and articles published in journals and periodicals of other organizations (list available).

CHELONIA INSTITUTE
P.O. Box 9174
Arlington, Virginia 22209
703-524-4900

Founded in 1977. Works for the conservation of marine turtles through research, land acquisition, and dissemination of information. Contact: Robert W. Truland, Director.

CHIHUAHUAN DESERT RESEARCH INSTITUTE (CDRI)
P.O. Box 1334
Alpine, Texas 79830
915-837-2475

Formed in 1974 "to promote understanding and appreciation of the Chihuahuan Desert Region through scientific research and public education." The Chihuahuan Desert is a natural biotic province in northern Mexico and extending into Texas and adjacent parts of the southwestern U.S. CDRI cooperates in Mexican conservation efforts, for example in gathering data to support proposals for wildlife refuges. Contact: Dennis J. Miller, Executive Director. Pub: THE CHIHUAHUAN DESERT DISCOVERY, semiannual.

CHILDREN OF THE GREEN EARTH
Star Route, Box 182
Umpqua, Oregon 97486
503-459-3122

Founded in 1980 by Rene Dubos, Richard St. Barbe Baker, and Dorothy Maclean to help children plant trees and do other "earth healing work" in the U.S. and abroad. Groups are also active in Europe, Australia, New Zealand. Contact: Ron Rabin or Michael Soule.

CLARK UNIVERSITY
INTERNATIONAL DEVELOPMENT PROGRAM
Worcester, Massachusetts 01610
617-793-7201

Research and educational activities of Clark's Program for International Development and Social Change focused on Africa during the '70s, but have recently been expanded to include Central America and South and Southeast Asia. The Program's Center for Technology, Environment, and Development emphasizes resource management and planning, including problems of desertification, soil erosion, water quality, environmental health, urban pollution, and land use. Holds courses and seminars in Africa. Collaborates with the University of North Carolina and the South-East Consortium for International Development in the Environmental Training and Management in Africa (ETMA) project. Pub: NETWORK FOR ENVIRONMENT AND DEVELOPMENT, periodic bulletin. Reports.

THE CONSERVATION FOUNDATION (CF)
1717 Massachusetts Avenue, N.W.
Washington, D.C. 20036
202-797-4300

"A nonprofit research organization committed to improving the quality of the environment and promoting wise use of the earth's resources, The Conservation Foundation conducts interdisciplinary research and communicates its findings to policymakers and other influential audiences." A non-membership organization, CF has a staff that includes lawyers, economists, scientists, political scientists, urban planners, resource management specialists, and experts in other fields. It was founded in 1948. "During the past three decades, as awareness of the environment has grown in the United States, The Conservation Foundation has continually adapted its program to meet emerging needs. In its early years, the Foundation served as prophet, alerting the nation and the world to environmental dangers: population growth, water shortages, diminishing wildlife in Africa, soil erosion, and misuse of pesticides. More recently, the Foundation has helped to build and implement a national legislative program to protect the environment. Currently, it concentrates on seeking practical ways to reconcile potentially conflicting public objectives, so that immediate needs such as energy and economic development may be satisfied without sacrificing the nation's environment and resource base."

The Conservation Foundation has three priorities for the 1980s: (1) demonstrating the importance of resource conservation, especially of energy and agricultural resources, to the long-term health and well-being of the United States and the world; (2) consolidating gains in environmental programs, particularly working to improve their cost-effectiveness; and (3) encouraging state, local, and private initiatives in addressing resource and environmental concerns.

Most of CF's work focuses on problems in the U.S., but there are also important projects on international aspects of resource management. The major international activity in recent years has been the International Comparative Land-Use Project (ICLUP), which started in 1974. It looks at the programs of foreign countries for "practical ideas and techniques to resolve land-use and environmental management problems confronting the United States." Research has been conducted principally in Australia, West Germany, France, the United Kingdom, Israel, Japan, Mexico, and the Netherlands.

In 1978-80, the Foundation conducted an Industrial Siting Project to investigate domestic industrial plant siting disputes and innovative siting processes; the environmental impacts of the concentration or dispersion of industry in the U.S. and abroad; and the impact of growing environmental awareness abroad on efforts by multilateral corporations to site new industrial developments in industrializing countries. In 1979-80, CF prepared an international primer on toxic substances control to analyze the manner in which variations among nations' approaches to controlling toxic substances may hinder or encourage economic development and the protection of public health and the environment.

"Other Foundation projects...have benefited from the expertise and perspectives developed during the course of international comparative research, as well as from institutional and governmental contacts resulting from staff visits abroad."

Contact: William K. Reilly, President. Pub: CONSERVATION FOUNDATION LETTER, a topical monthly report on environmental issues. Books; reports; films.

COORDINATION IN DEVELOPMENT, INC. (CODEL)
79 Madison Avenue
New York, New York 10157
212-685-2030

CODEL is a consortium of some 40 U.S.-based organizations working in development assistance abroad; almost all of them are church-related, and most are Roman Catholic. CODEL's Environment and Development Program works to assist all private voluntary agencies involved in small-scale development projects in Third-World countries "in incorporating environmental considerations into the planning, implementation, and monitoring of projects." It offers training and informational materials, and operates as a clearinghouse in the field. Contact: Helen L. Vukasin or Carol Roever. Pub: CODEL NEWS, bimonthly. Handbooks, including ENVIRONMENTALLY SOUND SMALL SCALE DEVELOPMENT PROJECTS, and ENVIRONMENTALLY SOUND SMALL-SCALE FORESTRY PROJECTS.

COUNCIL FOR INTERNATIONAL URBAN LIAISON
818 18th Street, N.W., Room 840
Washington, D.C. 20006
202-223-1434

Organized in the late '70s by the principal local government associations of the U.S. and Canada "to operate an international clearinghouse of practical experience in dealing with the common urban problems that beset all industrialized nations." The main vehicles for this effort are two newsletters, URBAN INNOVATION ABROAD, monthly; and URBAN TRANSPORTATION ABROAD, quarterly. Environmental topics are regularly covered in both publications. Contact: George G. Wynne, Director of Communications.

THE COUSTEAU SOCIETY, INC.
930 W. 21st Street
Norfolk, Virginia 23517
804-627-1144

Founded in 1973 by Captain Jacques-Yves Cousteau. A "non-profit membership-supported organization dedicated to the protection and improvement of life." Principal themes are the ocean environment and water quality. Carries on research; produces films, filmstrips, and television programs. Sponsors Ocean Search Expeditions, in cooperation with the University of Southern California, in which members of the public may join. Contributes to marine policy through studies, testimony, and participation in international conferences. Plans a Cousteau Ocean Center in Norfolk, Virginia. Membership of 200,000 is concentrated in the U.S. and France. Pub: CALYPSO LOG, quarterly magazine. DOLPHIN LOG, quarterly magazine for children. Policy papers, e.g., BASIC PRINCIPLES FOR A GLOBAL OCEAN POLICY (1979); A BILL OF RIGHTS FOR FUTURE GENERATIONS (1980). Books.

CULTURAL SURVIVAL
11 Divinity Avenue
Cambridge, Massachusetts 02138
617-495-2562

Works to protect indigenous peoples and ethnic minorities, primarily in Latin
America, but also in other parts of the world. In many countries, there is a
close relationship between protection of natural areas and protection of
indigenous people. One recent project, for example, focused on legal rights of
Brazilian Indians in response to government attempts to develop alternative
energy sources. "One of the principal sources of energy now being developed is
hyrdroelectric power, but many Indians live either in or on the borders of the
areas to be flooded." Contact: David Maybury-Lewis, President. Pub: CULTURAL
SURVIVAL NEWSLETTER, quarterly. Occasional papers and special reports, e.g.,
BRAZIL-SPECIAL REPORT; THE CERRO COLORADO COPPER PROJECT AND THE GUAYNU INDIANS
OF PANAMA. Slide shows.

EARTHWATCH
10 Juniper Road, Box 127
Belmont, Massachusetts 02178
617-489-3030

EARTHWATCH, founded in 1971, and with 13,000 members, serves as a clearinghouse
matching scientists who need volunteers and funds with amateurs interested in
sharing the work and costs of field expeditions throughout the world.
EARTHWATCH's goal is "to encourage public participation and understanding of
both cultural and scientific research." Participants join small (6-15 member)
research teams under the direction of prominent scholars in the earth, life, and
marine sciences and the humanities. About 75 expeditions are sponsored each
year. They last for 10 days to a month. While scientific research is the main
purpose of the program, some of the trips are closely related to conservation
goals. For example, expeditions have looked into the plight of the iguana in
the Caribbean; gathered data needed to protect fishes of the tropical
rainforest along the Pacific coast of Costa Rica; and done research on the
humpback whales of the Pacific Ocean. Field offices in Los Angeles, Seattle,
Australia, Kenya, and England. Contact: Brian Rosborough, President. Pub:
Catalogs and notices of new expeditions.

EAST-WEST CENTER
1777 East-West Road
Honolulu, Hawaii 96848
General number: 808-944-7111

The East-West Center, officially known as the Center for Cultural and Technical
Interchange Between East and West, is a national educational institution
established in Hawaii by the U.S. Congress in 1960 to promote better relations
and understanding between the U.S. and the nations of Asia and the Pacific
through cooperative study, training, and research. "Each year, more than 1500
men and women from many nations and cultures participate in Center programs that
seek cooperative solutions to problems of mutual consequence to East and West.
Working with the Center's multicultural and multidisciplinary staff,
participants include visiting scholars and researchers; leaders and
professionals from the academic, government, and business communities; and
graduate degree students. Pub: EAST-WEST PERSPECTIVES, quarterly magazine.
Annual catalog of publications in print.

Two of the Center's five problem-oriented institutes deal with international environmental and resource issues. These are the East-West Environmental and Policy Institute (EAPI), and the East-West Resource Systems Institute (RSI). In addition, a joint Research Materials Center serves information needs of both centers. Each of these three units is described separately below:

East-West Environment and Policy Institute (EAPI)
(808-944-7266)

EAPI "explores how many sectors affect the environment and how the environmental dimension can be integrated into the consideration of the policies. It seeks to develop and apply alternatives available to decisionmakers and in assessing the implications of such choices. In the broadest sense, EAPI studies deal with the utilization of parts of the natural environment - land, air, forest, fresh water, and oceans, and the living and nonliving resources on and in them. A variety of policies, such as those related to economic development and energy strategies, are analyzed to illuminate their dependence and impacts on natural systems and thus on the objectives of the policies.

"There is a major emphasis in EAPI on the assessment of scientific and technical information on natural systems that is needed for more coherent policy formulation and implementation. Through analysis of many different situations, the Institute should provide insights into new and creative ways of dealing with conflicts between the goals of a society and the ability of natural systems to respond to them."

EAPI's work is conducted within and across four interrelated projects:

-- Natural Systems Assessment for Development Project. Focuses on assisting policy and decision makers with economic development that is based on, or affects, natural systems. Improved methods are being sought to assemble, analyze, and display scientific information about land/water systems so that productive uses may be sustainable. Benefit-cost analysis is being extended to explicitly identify and evaluate all significant natural systems factors in selecting among alternative development strategies.

-- Human Interactions with Tropical Ecosystems Project. Seeks to better understand the complex interactions between people and the tropical ecosystems that support them. This will provide the knowledge base needed for development of improved systems of environmental management. The principal areas of concentration are human ecology research on tropical agroecosystems, analysis of agroforestry practices, and investigations of watershed-forest influences. Southeast Asia has been a major focus of this project.

-- Marine Environment and Extended Marine Jurisdictions Project. Provides an independent, informal forum for specific identification and exchange of views on evolving East-West ocean management questions. Research is designed to provide a knowledge base of scientific and technical information to aid in the international understanding of these issues. An atlas of marine policy parameters has been prepared to provide research findings in graphic and cartographic formats that may be useful in cooperative, common, and national policy decisions. Other areas of work include transnational arrangements for fish stocks, energy material transportation, and transnational oil and gas resource management issues.

-- Environmental Dimensions of Energy Policies Project. Focuses on exploring how the natural resource and environmental bases of different countries affect, and are affected by, the formulation of national and international policies for energy. Other goals are assessment of the adequacy of scientific and economic data required for informed decisionmaking, and examination of methodologies that could be used for the comprehensive planning of energy-environment policies.

Contact: William H. Matthews, Director. Pub: ENVIRONMENT AND POLICY, newsletter. Annual program announcement. Research Reports series, e.g., ENVIRONMENTAL MANAGEMENT IN THE SOUTH CHINA SEA (1982). Reprint series. Books; program reports; workshop reports. Catalog available.

East-West Resource Systems Institute (RSI)
(808-944-7505)

The program of RSI is "directed to the overall goal of how nations can maintain adequate, equitable, and reliable access to resources. This effort is intended to explore the feasibility, advantages, and costs of moving the resource systems of the East-West area toward greater stability and resilience... The problems of resources are intimately linked with the concepts of both 'stability,' which is needed for the present good, and with 'resilience,' which is needed for the future good. A basic need, then, both national and international, is to learn how to manage the global resource system in such a way as to maximize stability and resilience."

RSI's work is conducted within and across three interrelated projects:

-- Food Systems Project. Conducts research on the institutional and policy aspects of improving food security in the Asia-Pacific region.

-- Energy Systems Project. Provides analyses of the vulnerabilities of nations to disruptions in the flow of fuels; collects and analyzes data on energy supply, demand, and flow, especially those in rural areas; evaluates alternative development policies on a variety of energy systems; and develops energy indexing methodologies and information exchange both within and among nations.

-- Raw Materials Systems Project. Concerned with evaluating policy options that will benefit nations from the exploration and development of their mineral resource potential.

Contact: Harrison Brown, Director. Pub: RSI, quarterly newsletter. Books and monographs.

Research Materials Center (RMC)

RMC is the central source for filling the informational needs for both EAPI and RSI. Individual collections held by those two institutes were "consolidated in 1979 into a single, coherent system supervised by experienced and professionally trained information specialists." Main subject areas are energy systems, food systems, natural systems assessment, raw materials systems, and the marine environment. "The RMC encourages exchange of information and use of its collection by institutions and countries throughout the Asian-Pacific region." Pub: Acquisition lists and bibliographies.

ECOLOGICAL SOCIETY OF AMERICA
Office of the Business Manager
Department of Botany and Microbiology
Arizona State University
Tempe, Arizona 85281
602-965-3000

Organized in 1915, the Society represents professional and academic ecologists
in North America. It has about 6500 members who are largely involved with
academic research and teaching. Ecological research in other countries is
regularly reported in Society publications. U.S. affiliate of the International
Association for Ecology (INTECOL). Committee on Coordination has a subcommittee
concerned with INTECOL and works to further joint programs and other
relationships with other ecological and environmental organizations inside and
outside North America. Pub: ECOLOGY, bimonthly. ECOLOGICAL MONOGRAPHS.
BULLETIN.

ELSA WILD ANIMAL APPEAL (EWAA)
P.O. Box 4572
North Hollywood, California 91607
213-769-8388

Founded in 1966 by Joy Adamson, author of BORN FREE and other books about
African wildlife. Dedicated to the conservation of all wildlife, protection of
endangered species and the natural environment, establishment of wildlife
sanctuaries, and support for educational and research projects. Affiliated with
EWAA groups in Canada, Japan, Kenya, and the United Kingdom. Contact: A. Peter
Rasmussen, Jr., General Manager.

ENVIRONMENTAL DEFENSE FUND (EDF)
444 Park Avenue South
New York, New York 10016
212-686-4191

EDF is a major national environmental organization, founded in 1967 and with
some 46,000 members. The organization's focus is on domestic issues. However,
EDF's Wildlife Program has for several years, with funding from the World
Wildlife Fund-U.S., provided legal and scientific expertise to WWF-US, other
U.S. conservation organizations, and occasionally international bodies to
monitor the implementation of U.S. laws that pertain to international
conservation of wildlife and wildlife habitat. It also advocates measures to
improve the effectiveness of those laws in administrative, judicial, and
legislative forums. Particular concerns are U.S. obligations under the
Convention on International Trade in Endangered Species (CITES) and the
Convention on the Conservation of Antarctic Living Marine Resources. EDF has
also been active in securing legislative reathorization of the U.S. Endangered
Species Act. Contact: Michael J. Bean, Chairman, Wildlife Program. Pub: THE
ASSOCIATE, quarterly. EDF LETTER, bimonthly.

ENVIRONMENTAL RESEARCH AND TECHNOLOGY, INC. (ERT)
696 Virginia Road
Concord, Massachusetts 01742
617-369-8910

ERT, a subsidiary of the Communications Satellite Corporation (COMSAT), is a
commercial environmental consulting and technical services firm. The
International Environmental Management Institute, ERT's professional education
division, has been offering an annual International Seminar on Environmental
Resources and Environmental Management in Developing Countries. The Seminar is
a two-week "integration of the key administrative, scientific, technical, legal,
economic, social, industrial, and training aspects of resource and environmental
management. Presentations are made by among the world's leading practicing
experts...including visiting faculty from the United Nations and the World Bank.
Participants analyze and discuss actual case studies and make field visits to
municipal and industrial sites." By 1983, the Seminar has included over 120
participants from more than 30 countries and 6 international organizations.

FORUM INTERNATIONAL: INTERNATIONAL ECOSYSTEMS UNIVERSITY
2702 Fulton Street
Berkeley, California 94705
415-843-8294

Founded in 1965 to realize, on a decentralized global basis, the International
Ecosystems University, "the first transdisciplinary and 'whole earth' oriented
institution of higher education." Representatives are also active in Austria,
France, and Italy. Contact: Nicholas D. Hetzer, Director. Pub: ECOSPHERE,
newsletter.

FRIENDS OF AFRICA IN AMERICA
330 S. Broadway
Tarrytown, New York 10591
914-631-5168

Founded in 1963; promotes understanding of the development problems of African
countries and support for wildlife conservation, particularly in East Africa.
Contact: Clement E. Merowit, President.

FRIENDS OF THE EARTH (FOE)
1045 Sansome Street
San Francisco, California 94111
415-433-7373

Friends of the Earth, "an activist environmental lobbying organization," is
"committed to the preservation, restoration, and rational use of the earth." It
was founded in 1969 by David R. Brower, and currently has some 32,000 members.
International issues have been a major concern, particularly those related to
nuclear power and alternate energy sources, marine mammals, the world oceans,
and wilderness. FOE has published ECO, an unofficial newspaper for delegates,
observers, and press, at such international meetings as the United Nations
conferences on environment and food, and meetings of the International Atomic
Energy Agency. Affiliated Friends of the Earth groups exist in some 20
countries, ranging from Les Amis de la Terre in France to Amigos de la Tierra in

Mexico. Contact: Jeffrey Knight, Executive Director; David Chatfield,
International Representative. Washington office: 530 7th Street, S.E.,
Washington, D.C. 20003, 202-543-4312. Pub: NOT MAN APART, monthly newspaper.
Books and reports.

The International Project for Soft Energy Paths, same address, was organized in
1978 to "report rapidly and accurately on the technical and economic
characteristics of 'soft' technologies being developed worldwide, in large part
by groups unconnected with national energy research organizations." Contact:
Jim Harding, Director. Pub: SOFT ENERGY NOTES, bimonthly.

GEORGETOWN UNIVERSITY
CENTER FOR STRATEGIC AND INTERNATIONAL STUDIES (CSIS)
1800 K Street, N.W.
Washington, D.C. 20006
202-887-0200

Recent activities have included a number of projects related to global
environmental and resource management issues, e.g., "Mexico and Energy," and
"Food and Foreign Policy." In 1980, the Center published a policy paper in its
"The Washington Papers" series about the Green Movement in Western Europe
("Ecological Politics: The Rise of the Green Movement," by J.F. Pilat). Pub:
THE WASHINGTON QUARTERLY. THE WASHINGTON PAPERS, eight per year.

GLOBAL TOMORROW COALITION (GTC)
1525 New Hampshire Avenue, N.W.
Washington, D.C. 20036
202-328-8222

The Global Tomorrow Coalition, founded in 1981, is a "non-profit, publicly-
supported U.S. coalition of more than 60 organizations with combined memberships
of over 6,000,000 Americans. Coalition members share a concern for long-range
global issues, including population, resources, environment, sustainable
development, conservation, wildlife protection, species diversity,
deforestation, food production and distribution, health, and public education.
With a small central staff, assisted by volunteers, the Coalition works through
its members to broaden public understanding in the U.S. of the long-term
significance of interrelated global and national trends, and to promote timely
choice among alternative policies and actions to ensure a more sustainable and
equitable future."

GTC was founded "to a large extent" in response to THE GLOBAL 2000 REPORT TO THE
PRESIDENT, released in 1980. "GLOBAL 2000 was the first effort by a major
national government to draw upon its own data resources to sketch the outline of
the world we may live in at the end of this century if present trends and
policies proceed unchanged."

The Global Tomorrow Coalition "believes that we need (1) to gain a better
understanding of global trends and their interactions over time; (2) to define
clearly the goals - social, economic, political, ethical, environmental, and
cultural - toward which policy changes in the U.S. should be directed; (3) to
reach broad public consensus as soon as possible on how those goals are to be
achieved in a representative democracy; and (4) to take timely action to assure
a more sustainable future."

In Washington, D.C., Coalition staff and representatives of member organizations work with policy makers in government and the private sector "to encourage decisions responsive to the needs of tomorrow, and in particular to develop an improved capacity for 'national foresight' in our government and society." Holds meetings in Washington and at the community level across the country. Has task forces on biological diversity, coastal and marine resources, nuclear war and global survival, information and education, national foresight capacity, population, tropical forests, and water resources.

Many of the organizations listed in this book are members of the Global Tomorrow Coalition. Among them, for example, are the Center for Law and Social Policy, Conservation Foundation, Environmental Defense Fund, Friends of the Earth, International Institute for Environment and Development, National Audubon Society, National Wildlife Federation, Natural Resources Defense Council, New York Zoological Society, Oceanic Society, Rachel Carson Council, Sierra Club, Tufts University, and U.S. Association for the Club of Rome (a full list is available from GTC).

In June 1983, GTC held a major conference in Washington, "Global Resources, Environment and Population: Rebuilding United States Leadership," at which former President Jimmy Carter was the keynote speaker. Contact: Donald R. Lesh, Executive Director. Pub: INTERACTION, newsletter.

GREENPEACE, USA, INC.
2007 R Street, N.W.
Washington, D.C. 20009
202-462-1177

Founded in 1970 and best known for employing non-violent direct action to confront environmental abuse. Has 280,000 active supporters. Currently, its first priority is to work for an international treaty to ban the testing of nuclear weapons. Other projects include working to halt dumping of nuclear and other toxic wastes in the oceans through direct confrontation with dumpers; protection of whales, seals, and kangaroos; working to designate Antarctica as a global park; and conferences and dialogues in several countries on the problem of acid rain. Contact: Chris Cook, Administrator. Pub: THE GREENPEACE EXAMINER, quarterly. Books and booklets, e.g., POLLUTION OF THE NORTH SEA; WARRIORS OF THE RAINBOW; VOYAGE OF THE GREENPEACE III.

GULF AND CARIBBEAN FISHERIES INSTITUTE
4600 Rickenbacker Causeway
Miami. Florida 33149
305-350-7533

Founded in 1948; promotes research on and sound management of the fisheries of the Caribbean region and the Gulf of Mexico through annual meetings of scientists, government officials, and fishing industry representatives; information dissemination; and assistance to Caribbean countries in the development of their fisheries. Contact: James B. Higman, Executive Director. Pub: Proceedings of the annual meeting.

INTERNATIONAL CENTER FOR THE SOLUTION OF ENVIRONMENTAL PROBLEMS (ICSEP)
3818 Graustark
Houston, Texas 77006
713-527-8711

A non-profit organization "founded for the purpose of detecting upcoming
environmental problems and providing solutions for avoiding or reducing them.
The principal activity of the Center is to identify and clarify those
environmental problems that are caused by human activities worldwide, and to
suggest and demonstrate solutions in detail. The Center generally uses
recognized research and education institutions for both of these aspects of its
aims, in preference to setting up special in-house grouping." Particular areas
of interest are weather and climate change, and "the ill effects on weather, on
land, and on humans and other living organisms that result from excessive
deforestation and from over-grazing." Projects conducted or planned focus on
the Houston area, the Middle East, and South Asia. Works through a network of
24 affilliates in various countries. Contact: Joseph L. Goldman, Technical
Director.

INTERNATIONAL COUNCIL FOR BIRD PRESERVATION (ICBP)
UNITED STATES SECTION
c/o Warren B. King, Chairman
871 Dolley Madison Boulevard
McLean, Virginia 22101
709-356-5439

The ICBP, founded in 1922 and headquartered in Cambridge, England, is the major
international organization concerned with protection of bird species. It
compiles data; identifies conservation problems and priorities; and promotes,
initiates, and coordinates conservation projects and international agreements.
The U.S. Section is one of some 65 national sections of ICBP.

INTERNATIONAL CRANE FOUNDATION
City View Road
Baraboo, Wisconsin 53913
608-356-9462

Works to preserve the world's 15 species of cranes through research, habitat
preservation, captive propagation, restocking, public education, and
international cooperation. Projects include work in the USSR, India, Japan, and
Korea. Contact: Joan Fordham, Administrator. Pub: THE BROLGA BUGLE,
quarterly (for members only).

INTERNATIONAL INSTITUTE FOR ENVIRONMENT AND DEVELOPMENT (IIED)
1319 F Street, N.W., Suite 800
Washington, D.C. 20004
202-462-0900

IIED, a nonprofit organization founded in 1971 with offices in Washington and
London, undertakes policy studies on issues of concern to international
institutions, national governments, and nongovernmental organizations. At
present, the Institute is especially concerned with the issues of "future
energy, the development of sufficient shelter and clean water for mankind, the
use of applied ecology as a management tool, and the environmental consequences

and sustainability of social and economic development, especially in the Third World."

IIED runs an international news and information service called Earthscan. It also operates a Joint Environmental Service with IUCN, and maintains close working relationships with nongovernmental organizations working in similar fields around the world. Under the Institute's Three-Year Plan of Work, 1982-85, the following programs are emphasized:

-- Environmental Planning and Management Program. Major activities have included an analysis of environmental procedures and guidelines governing development aid, and policy studies on a range of aspects of tropical forestry. IIED also supports the work of the Global Tomorrow Coalition (which see) and a newly-formed group of European organizations, Common Ground International, which brings together population-oriented and natural resource conservation leaders in a search for areas of active cooperation.

-- Human Settlements Program. This program "has now been running for six years. In this time it has shown how governments that concentrate on providing people with basic services and infrastructure and ensuring that the poor majorities have access to legal housing sites in cities are more successful in improving housing conditions than those governments that do not." The National Assessment Program, which assesses the effectiveness of housing and land and settlement policies in various countries, is being carried out in cooperation with national institutions in Argentina, India, Nigeria, and the Sudan, and examined some 30 countries by 1983. In this field, IIED is also doing research into the present and potential role of small towns and intermediate settlements in the development process. Studies have been completed in five regions. IIED monitors the extent to which major multilateral aid agencies support projects aimed at improving housing and living conditions. Seminars, symposia, and conferences are held in collaboration with various other organizations, including universities in North Carolina, Mexico, Chile, and Argentina.

-- Energy Program. "In many developing countries a small handful of people are trying to shape national energy policy out of a little information and a lot of expert advice from powerful sectoral interests. It is no wonder that energy planning in such countries frequently shows a strong bias towards some energy supply options at the expense of others that could provide a more balanced and sustainable development strategy." In this field, IIED has concentrated on improving the energy planning capacities and the energy information base of developing countries. Recent projects have included developing an energy conservation and renewable energy strategy for Pakistan; a major effort to find ways of developing better energy statistics in developing countries, especially for noncommercial fuels such as firewood and crop residues; and a European Economic Community seminar, "National Energy Planning and Management in Developing Countries." IIED's Energy Program has also been active in the areas of woodfuel commercialization and solar energy technology. Workshops are being held in several world regions on the opportunities or barriers to increased development of commercial markets for renewable energy and energy conservation in developing countries.

-- Applied Ecology Program. "Ecological theory in isolation is an insufficient guide to the management of renewable resources, pests, and disease, as it poses questions that are far wider than purely biological. Since 1979, IIED has established a reputation as an initiator in the application of mathematical ecology to environment and development problems." IIED's first effort in this area was its marine program (in cooperation with IUCN), which seeks to "answer some basic questions about the ability of the world's fish resources to withstand exploitation." Marine mammals, especially whales and seals, has also been dealt with. The marine program "has moved from an initial concentration on purely biological problems to one one economics and management." IIED's applied ecology group also works to develop scientific analysis and management strategies for Antarctica and the Southern Ocean. Particular concerns have been Antarctica's mineral resources, chiefly oil and gas, and promoting broader public understanding of activities of the Antarctic Treaty System.

-- Earthscan. Headquartered at IIED's London office, with a bureau in Washington, Earthscan is an international news and information service. Environment- and development-oriented news articles are now distributed twice a week to over 120 newspapers in 60 countries in English, French, Spanish, and German. Briefing packets provide journalists with detailed background information on current global environment and resource issues. The EARTHSCAN BULLETIN carries shortened versions of Earthscan features and briefing documents to its network of environmental and development organizations, as well as TV and radio producers. Other activities include field trips for journalists (e.g., in Niger in 1982); press seminars at international conferences (e.g., at the Third World National Parks Congress in Indonesia in 1982); and a newsletter on the UN Water and Sanitation Decade, WATERLOG. A special research unit on alternative energy strategies was established in 1982. Earthscan has been highlighting issues related to deserts and desertification, the Caribbean region, water and sanitation, genetic resources, and energy.

-- Joint Environmental Service (JES). The JES is a cooperative effort between IIED and the International Union for Conservation of Nature and Natural Resources (IUCN; see separate entry). Its goal is "to help developing countries create or strengthen institutions, legal frameworks, and methodologies that will improve their ability to employ environmentally sound land-use planning and environmental assessment of proposed development schemes and projects." It will carry out this goal in three ways: (1) help in providing the right expertise, e.g., through a comprehensive roster of experts experienced in development planning as it affects natural resource use and conservation, and by sending missions to developing countries; (2) assistance in evolving national conservation strategies that follow the methodology of the WORLD CONSERVATION STRATEGY (see index); and (3) improving the state-of-the-art in natural resource planning and management, "a commitment to publish both technical papers and examinations of broader issues emanating from the evolution of national conservation strategies and the experience of the roster of advisory consultants."

Contact: David Runnalls, Director, Washington Office. Pub: Books and reports. Earthscan also issues audiovisual materials and publishes newsletters for special audiences (see description of Earthscan program above).

INTERNATIONAL PRIMATE PROTECTION LEAGUE (IPPL)
P.O. Drawer X
Summerville, South Carolina 29483
803-871-2280

Devoted to the conservation and protection of nonhuman primates. Founded in 1974. Contact: Shirley McGreal, Chairperson. Pub: IPPL NEWSLETTER, quarterly.

INTERNATIONAL STUDIES ASSOCIATION (ISA)
ENVIRONMENTAL STUDIES SECTION
c/o Professor Marvin S. Soroos, Chairman
Department of Political Science
North Carolina State University
Raleigh, North Carolina 27607
919-737-2481

The ISA is an organization of scholars concerned with international affairs.
The Environmental Studies Section, which has some 75 members, was organized in
1977 to "seek a better understanding of the interaction between natural and
human systems within global, regional, and national contexts" and "promote an
increased awareness among social and natural scientists and policy-makers of the
implications of environmental/ecological perspectives and global environmental
trends." Organizes panels and workshops at the annual ISA meeting. Contact:
Marvin S. Soroos, Chairman. Pub: NEWSLETTER, about 3 times a year.

INTERNATIONAL UNION FOR CONSERVATION OF NATURE AND NATURAL RESOURCES (IUCN)
Avenue du Mont-Blanc
1196 Gland, Switzerland
(022) 64 71 81

IUCN, founded in 1948, is the umbrella organization of the world conservation
movement. Its members are the governments of 57 countries; 118 governmental
agencies; and over 300 non-governmental organizations. Closely allied with the
World Wildlife Fund, which IUCN set up in 1961 to raise funds for its projects,
IUCN "monitors the status of ecosystems and species throughout the world; plans
conservation action, both at the strategic level and at the program level
through its program of "Conservation for Sustainable Development;" promotes such
action by governments, intergovernmental bodies, and non-governmental
organizations; and provides assistance and advice necessary for the achievement
of such action." In 1980, IUCN issued the WORLD CONSERVATION STRATEGY, a
widely-publicized document that outlines the need to work toward "ensuring
earth's capacity to sustain development and to support all life" and calls for
"global coordinated efforts backed by will and determination, for concerted
action at national and international levels, and for global solidarity to
implement its programs."

The United States is not a "State Member" of IUCN, but the U.S. Environmental
Protection Agency, U.S. Forest Service, and U.S. Department of the Interior
(National Park Service and U.S. Fish and Wildlife Service) are "government
agency" members. Some 50 non-governmental organizations in the U.S. are also
members. These include many of the organizations listed in this book, but also
a number of groups involved primarily with domestic or scientific problems that
affiliate with IUCN as an expression of their support for world conservation
efforts.

A good number of Americans are members of IUCN's six technical commissions:
Ecology; Education; Environmental Planning; Environmental Policy, Law, and
Administration; National Parks and Protected Areas; and Species Survival.
The IUCN Commission on Education has an Eastern U.S. Committee.

The American Committee for International Conservation (see separate listing)
serves to bring together many of the U.S. IUCN members based on the East Coast.

ISLAND RESOURCES FOUNDATION
Red Hook Center, Box 33
St. Thomas, Virgin Islands 00801
809-775-3225

Founded in 1971 and "dedicated to improved resource planning, management, and development strategies for small tropical islands." Projects focus on the Caribbean and Latin America. Examples of activities related to natural resources include marine park planning in the British Virgin Islands; a "Caribbean Cruise in Conservation and Preservation;" and Caribbean sea turtle research and conservation. Contact: Edward L. Towle, President. Washington office: Webster House, Suite L-8, 1718 P Street, N.W., Washington, D.C. 20036, 202-265-9712. Pub: BULLETIN, semi-annual; books and reports.

JAPANESE-AMERICAN ENVIRONMENTAL CONFERENCES
c/o Claude A. Look, Secretary
411 Los Ninos Way
Los Altos, California 94022
415-968-4509

Sponsors a series of biennial conferences of American and Japanese environmental leaders, specialists, and officials to discuss issues of mutual concern. The first conference was held in Japan in 1978. The second was held in 1980 in California at separate sessions in San Diego and at Stanford University. The third was held in 1982 in Japan. Topics have included the impact of development on parks and scenery; disposal of hazardous wastes; rare and over-abundant species; deep sea mining; coastal planning; and marine mammal and fisheries issues. Pub: Conference proceedings.

LAW OF THE SEA INSTITUTE
University of Hawaii
2540 Dole Street, Holmes 401
Honolulu, Hawaii 96822
808-948-6750

Formerly located at the University of Rhode Island. "Serves as a means for the exchange of knowledge and ideas concerning the uses of the sea and its resources...The principal emphasis is on the international law of the seas as it now exists and as it may be expected to evolve in years to come." Natural resource management has been a major theme. Holds annual conferences in cities around the world. Holds workshops on various topics, e.g., "Arctic Ocean Issues in the 1980s," and "Law of the Sea: Major Problems from the East Asian Perspective." Pub: Conference proceedings; workshop books; papers and bibliographies.

LOUISIANA STATE UNIVERSITY
LATIN AMERICAN STUDIES INSTITUTE
Baton Rouge, Louisiana 70803

Includes a special program, in cooperation with LSU's Center for Wetlands Resources, which is studying the ecological impact of coastlines and inland waterways on populations in Latin America. This program "seeks to bridge technical developments in the marine sciences and their comparative effect on human problems within the framework of U.S. mainland experience." Contact: Roland E. Chardon, Director.

L.S.B. LEAKEY FOUNDATION
Foundation Center 13-83
Pasadena, California 91125
213-449-0507

Established in 1968 "by a group of eminent scientists and informed laymen who recognized a critical need to strengthen financial support for new multi-disciplined research into man's origins, his evolving nature, and his environmental future. It was named in honor of the man who had become known as the 'Darwin of pre-history,' Dr. Louis S.B. Leakey" (1903-1972). Headquarters are at the California Institute of Technology. An important concern is the protection of apes, orangutans, chimpanzees, and other primates in their natural habitats. Has given active support to the World Wildlife Fund's major campaign to preserve tropical forests. Pub: THE L.S.B. LEAKEY FOUNDATION NEWS, quarterly.

MARINE TECHNOLOGY SOCIETY (MTS)
1730 M Street, N.W., Suite 412
Washington, D.C. 20036
202-659-3251

MTS, founded in 1963, is "concerned with the application of science and technology to the exploration and utilization of the oceans. It embraces the institutional, environmental, and social, as well as the physical and biological aspects of marine activities. As the leading marine-oriented interdisciplinary organization, its members and officials include outstanding scientists, educators, engineers, economists, attorneys, and the interested public." Largely a U.S. organization, the Society also has regional sections in Canada. Some 25 "Professional Panels" include Marine Fisheries, Marine Food and Drug Resources, Marine Law and Policy, Marine Mineral Resources, Ocean Economic Potential, Ocean Energy, and Water Quality. MTS facilitates the exchange of information on public and technical issues, and serves as a "focal point for disseminating information to young people, for maintaining close liaison with federal, state, and local officials on policy questions, and for publishing reports on current research, technological developments, and ocean policy. Contact: George K. Gowans, Executive Director. Pub: MARINE TECHNOLOGY SOCIETY JOURNAL. MTS NEWSLETTER. Conference proceedings.

MASSACHUSETTS INSTITUTE OF TECHNOLOGY
CENTER FOR INTERNATIONAL STUDIES
292 Main Street, Room E38-642
Cambridge, Massachusetts 02142
617-253-8070

The MIT Center for International Studies conducts research and analysis on international policy issues that have "significant technological aspects." Environmental problems have received considerable attention for some years. Studies have focused on the United Nations Environment Programme (UNEP), ocean oil pollution, social implications of climate changes, and damage to the ozone layer. The Center has also had an interest in energy, food, toxic chemical, and international development questions. Contact: Eugene B. Skolnikoff, Director. Pub: Research reports and working papers.

MONITOR
1506 19th Street, N.W.
Washington, D.C. 20036
202-234-6576

A consortium of 35 conservation, environmental, and animal welfare organizations that acts as a coordinating center and information clearinghouse for its member groups on issues concerning protection of endangered species and marine mammals. Does not offer services or information directly to the public. Contact: Craig Van Note, Executive Vice President.

NATIONAL AUDUBON SOCIETY
950 Third Avenue
New York, New York 10022
212-832-3200

One of the oldest and largest conservation organizations in the U.S., National Audubon, founded in 1905, has some 450,000 members. While its many research, educational, and action programs are focused mainly on the U.S., Audubon is also actively concerned with global environmental issues. Officers and staff participate in U.S. coalitions and in such international organizations as the International Union for Conservation of Nature and Natural Resources (IUCN); the American Committee for International Conservation (ACIC); the meetings of the International Whaling Commission; and the U.S.-Mexico Joint Wildlife Committee. Contact: Russell W. Peterson, President. Pub: AUDUBON, bimonthly magazine, which regularly includes articles on international issues. Specalized periodicals. Occasional reports on international topics.

NATIONAL CENTER FOR ATMOSPHERIC RESEARCH (NCAR)
P.O. Box 3000
Boulder, Colorado 80307
303-494-5151

NCAR's Environmental and Social Impacts Group has conducted studies on the social, political, and economic repercussions of the oceanographic-meteorological phenomenon El Nino on the Pacific Coast of the Americas; desertification in the Sahel region of Africa; societal impacts of climate variation on world food systems; and the environmental and societal impacts of a potential carbon dioxide-induced climate change. Contact: Michael H. Glantz, Head, Environmental and Social Impacts Group. Pub: Papers published as NCAR technical publications. Articles and books published by other organizations.

NATIONAL PARKS AND CONSERVATION ASSOCIATION (NPCA)
1701 18th Street, N.W.
Washington, D.C. 20009
202-265-2717

A major national conservation organization, founded in 1919, with 45,000
members. Focus is on the preservation, promotion, and improvement of the U.S.
National Park System. Though international problems have not been an important
concern, NPCA's board of trustees maintains an International Committee to work
on international park issues. Contact: Paul C. Pritchard, President. Pub:
NATIONAL PARKS, monthly magazine.

NATIONAL RESEARCH COUNCIL (NRC)
2101 Constitution Avenue, N.W.
Washington, D.C. 20418
202-393-8100

The National Research Council is the principal operating arm of the National
Academy of Sciences, the National Academy of Engineering, and the Institute of
Medicine, all of which are private, self-perpetuating societies of distinguished
scholars which are dedicated to furthering the use of their disciplines for
human welfare, and are obligated to advise the federal government, on request,
on matters related to their expertise.

The National Research Council (NRC) draws upon a wide cross-section of the
nation's leading scientists and engineers for advisory services to government
agencies and the Congress. It is organized into a complex structure of
commissions, offices, boards, committees, panels, and other units, many of which
are concerned with matters related to natural resource management and
environmental quality. The following units of the NRC are particularly
concerned with international environmental affairs:

-- Office of International Affairs (OIA). Conducts international programs
and examines relevant science policy issues, including those concerned with
scholarly communication, effective uses of science and technology in
development, and security and world peace. OIA is also responsible for
communication with other units of NRC to the extent that they are engaged in
international activities, and draws upon the science and technology resources of
the various NRC units for its programs. The primary objectives of OIA are (1)
to facilitate the participation of U.S. scientists in international
organizations and programs; (2) to enhance U.S. scientific cooperation and
exchanges with other countries; and (3) to engage the U.S. scientific community
in effective technical assistance to and cooperation with developing nations.

A major unit of the Office of International Affairs is the Board on Science and
Technology for International Development (BOSTID), which is responsible for
providing guidance for scientific and technical programs with developing
countries. It examines ways to apply science and technology to problems of
economic and social development through overseas bilateral programs, studies,
advisory committees, a research grants program, and other mechanisms. Working
with groups in developing countries, BOSTID's activities are aimed at
strengthening local science and technology capabilities in areas such as
agriculture, environment, natural resources, health, and energy; improving
organizational and planning capabilities; and suggesting possible scientific and
technological solutions to particular development problems.

BOSTID's subunits are the Advisory Committee on Technology Innovation; Advisory Committee on Health, Biomedical Research, and Development; Committee on Research Grants; U.S. Committee on Sino-American Science Cooperation (Taiwan); U.S.-Egypt Joint Consultative Committee; and Advisory Committee on the Sahel.

Representative recent BOSTID activities: sponsoring a symposium on biomass substitutes for liquid fuels in Brazil; a grant to the International Council for Research in Agroforestry in Kenya for research on fast-growing, nitrogen-fixing trees; an international workshop on priorities in biotechnology research for international development; work in the Sahel to increase the stability and productivity of agro-sylvo-pastoral systems; and a conference on development needs of Caribbean islands. Contact: John Hurley, Director, BOSTID. Pub: BOSTID DEVELOPMENTS, newsletter, 3 times a year.

Also under the Office of International Affairs are a number of U.S. national committees for international scientific bodies. These are the focal points for ensuring effective participation by American scientists in the work of the international organizations. Among them are the Advisory Committee for the International Council of Scientific Unions (AC/ICSU), which has a Subcommittee on UNESCO Science Programs.

-- Commission on Engineering and Technical Systems. Includes the Marine Board, whose concerns include ocean resource development.

-- Commission on Physical Sciences, Mathematics, and Resources. Several units of this Commission are interested in international resource problems. The Climate Board assesses research on climate change to assist the federal government in developing an effective climate research program; it has a Carbon Dioxide Assessment Committee. The Ocean Sciences Board and U.S. National Committee for the Scientific Committee on Ocean Research (SCOR) has projects on petroleum in the marine environment. The Ocean Policy Committee has organized a workshop on land versus sea disposal of industrial and domestic wastes. The Environmental Studies Board has a Joint U.S.-Canadian Scientific Committee on Acid Precipitation (with the Royal Society of Canada). Other units interested in international resource problems are the U.S. Committee for the Global Atmospheric Research Program (GARP, a joint project of the International Council of Scientific Unions and the World Meteorological Organization); and the Polar Research Board and U.S. National Committee on Antarctic Research.

Contact: Philip M. Smith, Executive Officer, National Research Council. Pub: NEWS REPORT, 10 times a year, reporting on current activities and summarizing recent publications of the National Academies, the Institute of Medicine, and the National Research Council. Numerous books and reports (catalog available from the National Academy Press, same address), e.g., ECOLOGICAL ASPECTS OF DEVELOPMENT IN THE HUMID TROPICS (1982); CARBON DIOXIDE AND CLIMATE: A SECOND ASSESSMENT (1982).

NATURAL RESOURCES DEFENSE COUNCIL (NRDC)
INTERNATIONAL PROJECT
1725 I Street, N.W., Suite 600
Washington, D.C. 20006
202-223-8210

Headquartered in New York, with some 45,000 members, NRDC is a major national environmental organization which has been particularly active in the areas of air and water pollution, control of toxic substances, offshore oil drilling, wildlife management, protection of natural areas, nuclear energy, forestry, and environmental impact assessment.

NRDC's International Project, based in Washington, D.C., is "active in two broad areas. First NRDC monitors and influences decisions of U.S. and international agencies affecting the international environment. Second, NRDC cooperates with and makes its expertise available to foreign environmental groups. NRDC's international activities are coordinated with those of other U.S. environmental groups and with NRDC's domestic efforts." Recent work has concentrated in the following areas:

-- Nuclear export policies and weapons proliferation. NRDC has worked to prevent the further spread of nuclear weapons by tightening controls on international nuclear commerce and limiting access to weapons-usable materials: plutonium and highly-enriched uranium.

-- Climatic and atmospheric change. This activity has focused on controlling the use of fluorocarbons, which deplete the earth's ozone layer; and on issues related to the buildup of carbon dioxide in the atmosphere due to combustion of fossil fuels and depletion of tropical forests.

-- Toxic substances, particularly harmonization of regulations in developed countries, and exports to developing countries.

-- Endangered species, concentrating on U.S. implementation of the Convention on International Trade in Endangered Species (CITES); enforcement of the U.S. Endangered Species Act; and requiring the U.S. Agency for International Development (USAID) to take into account protection of foreign endangered species in its activities.

-- Environmental impact assessment. Legal, legislative, and administrative action to require USAID and the U.S. Export-Import Bank to prepare environmental assessments for proposed actions significantly affecting the environment.

-- Environment and development. Requiring USAID to make "environmental protection an integral part of the development process."

-- Tropical moist forests, concentrating on information and education for decisionmakers, influencing the U.S. Government, and working with the International Union for Conservation of Nature and Natural Resources (IUCN).

Contact: Thomas B. Stoel, Jr., Director, International Project, in Washington. New York office: 122 E. 42nd Street, New York, New York 10168, 212-949-0049. Pub: NRDC publishes THE AMICUS JOURNAL, quarterly. The International Project issues books and reports, e.g., AIDING THE ENVIRONMENT: A STUDY OF THE ENVIRONMENTAL POLICIES, PROCEDURES, AND PERFORMANCE OF THE U.S. AGENCY FOR INTERNATIONAL DEVELOPMENT (1980).

NATIONAL WILDLIFE FEDERATION (NWF)
1412 Sixteenth Street, N.W.
Washington, D.C. 20036
202-797-6800

A major national conservation organization, founded in 1936. Its membership of
4.3 million includes the members of state affiliates, which in turn are largely
composed of local rod and gun clubs, as well as individual members. NWF
publishes a bimonthly magazine, INTERNATIONAL WILDLIFE, circulation 450,000,
which gives popular treatment to conservation issues around the world. For the
Canadian Wildlife Federation, NWF publishes a special edition of INTERNATIONAL
WILDLIFE with a Canadian insert. The Federation also has an arrangement with
the Japan Science Society to publish the magazine in Japanese.

NWF has an International Affairs Committee, which coordinates its involvement in
international conservation issues. Recent concerns have included monitoring
the work of the International Whaling Commission; wildlife treaties between the
U.S. and Canada; international aspects of acid precipitation, particularly
between the U.S. and Canada; ocean dumping; the Convention on International
Trade in Endangered Species (CITES); the Law of the Sea; and tropical forests.
Much of NWF's work on international issues is done through coalitions and
international organizations. Contact: Jay D. Hair, Executive Vice President.
Pub: NATIONAL WILDLIFE, bimonthly magazine. INTERNATIONAL WILDLIFE, bimonthly
magazine (see above). RANGER RICK'S NATURE MAGAZINE, children's monthly.
CONSERVATION REPORT, weekly legsilative newsletter while Congress is in session.
CONSERVATION DIRECTORY, annual. Pamphlets and other educational materials
(catalog available).

THE NATURE CONSERVANCY
INTERNATIONAL PROGRAM
1785 Massachusetts Avenue, N.W.
Washington, D.C. 20036
202-483-0231

The Nature Conservancy, founded in 1950, and with some 150,000 members, is a
national organization "committed to the preservation of natural diversity by
protecting lands containing the best examples of all components of our natural
world." It maintains a system of over 700 natural area sanctuaries throughout
the U.S.

"Conservation of living resources in countries outside the U.S. has always been
a Conservancy objective. The Conservancy's precursor organization, the
Ecological Society's Special Committee for the Preservation of Natural
Conditions, did not distinguish between conservation objectives in the U.S. and
elsewhere. The NATURALISTS' GUIDE TO THE AMERICAS, published by the Committee
in 1926, described ecological conditions from Greenland to the Amazon.

"From 1962 to 1969 the Conservancy maintained a 'Latin American Desk' through
which it attempted to aid and encourage the efforts of Conservancy-like
organizations elsewhere in the hemisphere. From 1974 until 1979, the
Conservancy's International Program took a more direct approach and concentrated
on assisting government angencies and local conservationists to protect a
variety of magnificent ecological reserves in Canada, the Caribbean, and
Central America."

In addition to various projects in Canada, the Conservancy's International
Program has worked to preserve areas on the Caribbean islands of Dominica and
Bonaire and in Costa Rica and Belize. In Central America, it "has been able to
help in small ways by raising funds and advising local groups on some of the
technical aspects of parkland acquisition."

Contact: F. William Burley, Director of Science, International Program. Pub:
The national organization issues THE NATURE CONSERVANCY NEWS bimonthly.

NEW YORK ZOOLOGICAL SOCIETY
The Zoological Park, 185th Street and Southern Boulevard
Bronx, New York 10460
212-220-5100

In addition to operating the Bronx Zoo, the New York Aquarium, and a marine
science laboratory, the NYZS conducts a major international conservation program
through its Animal Research and Conservation Center. The Society claims that
in this field "no other private conservation organization has a research program
conducted by a staff of comparable size and expertise; they strive to obtain a
better understanding of the structure, functioning, and stability of large
ecosystems and to apply this understanding to their conservation." NYZS
involvement in international conservation dates back to 1895.

Center priorities, which "reflect areas and topics often neglected by other
organizations," include (1) developing countries, especially those in which
little research has been conducted and where major problems exist (e.g., Brazil
and the Sudan); (2) large, threatened, but little-known habitats (e.g.,
rainforests and oceanic islands); (3) species and groups of species which
require urgent attention (e.g., crocodilians, primates, whales); and (4)
wildlife "spectacles" (large aggregations of birds, mammals, or other animals
concentrated into small areas) which are attractive to tourists and also
vulnerable to extermination.

Most of the Center's projects are designed to try to help local scientists and
conservation officials establish research priorities and management plans to
ensure protection of vital species and habitats. Representative projects in
recent years (typically, there are some 60 projects in half as many countries)
include work on sea and river turtles in Malaysia; endangered birds on
Mauritius; national park management in Kenya; monkeys in Brazil; and mountain
gorilla habitat in Rwanda, East Africa.

Contact: George Schaller, Director, Animal Research and Conservation Center.
Pub: The NYZS issues ANIMAL KINGDOM, a quarterly magazine. The Center
publishes a detailed biennial report.

THE OCEANIC SOCIETY
Stamford Marine Center
Magee Avenue
Stamford, Connecticut 06902
203-327-9786

Founded in 1969, with 70,000 members, The Oceanic Society is "devoted to the
preservation and protection of the marine environment through research,
education, and conservation programs." Addresses international marine
conservation issues "principally through convening public policy forums which

focus attention on critical issues." Has a continuing effort to incorporate recommendations of marine biologists in the process of shaping international management programs for living marine resources in the Southern Ocean surrounding Antarctica. Also concerned with analysis of U.S. policy on disposal of low- and high-level radioactive wastes in the marine environment within the context of international practices and regulations. Sponsors Cetacean Intelligence, an international scientific forum bringing together experts in cetacean and other forms of mammalian intelligence. Monitors "new directions in marine policy to identify emerging marine conservation issues." The Society also conducts study-recreational oceanic expeditions in various parts of the world. Western Regional Office at Building E, Fort Mason Center, San Francisco, California 94123, telephone 415-441-1104. Contact: Thomas C. Jackson, Vice President. Pub: OCEANS, bimonthly magazine. Books and reports, e.g., INTRODUCTION TO SOUTHERN OCEAN CONSERVATION ISSUES (1980); NUCLEAR WASTE MANAGEMENT: THE OCEAN ALTERNATIVE (1981). Films.

PACIFIC SEABIRD GROUP
P.O. Box 321
Bolinas, California 94924

Founded in 1974; promotes the knowledge, study, and conservation of Pacific seabirds. 415 members. Contact: Harry M. Ohlendorf, Chairman. Pub: PACIFIC SEABIRD GROUP BULLETIN.

PROJECT JONAH
Building 240, Fort Mason Center
San Francisco, California 94123
415-285-9846

Works to prevent the commercial and/or biological extinction of threatened Cetacean species (whales, dolphins, and related marine mammals) by changing public and governmental attitudes toward commercial and military uses. Conducts and encouranges live observational research with wild, free-living whales and dolphins. Contact: Joan McIntyre, Research Director.

RACHAEL CARSON COUNCIL
8940 Jones Mill Road
Chevy Chase, Maryland 20815
301-652-1877

Founded in 1965 as the Rachael Carson Trust for the Living Environment, Inc., as a memorial to the author of SILENT SPRING. Operates a "unique intelligence center on environmental problems and prospects" focused on "chemical contamination, especially the pesticide problem explored in SILENT SPRING... Takes an increasingly active role in efforts to deal with global environmental problems...through the assistance of our Sponsors and Experts in other countries and through our participation in international meetings and programs...Since the Stockholm Conference of 1972, we have had a key role in coordinating information and suggestions for the United Nations Environment Programme, for our U.S. delegation to their sessions, and in the topical meetings they have sponsored." Contact: Shirley A. Briggs, Executive Director. Pub: Reports and brochures. Book, THE CHEMICAL CLOUD THAT FELL ON SEVESO (1976), translations from the Italian press about the explosion of a chemical plant in Seveso, Italy.

RARE, INC.
950 Third Avenue
New York, New York 10022
212-546-9297

"RARE" stands for Rare Animal Relief Effort. The organization works to advance the protection of endangered species and habitat, mainly through conservation education and technical and financial assistance in developing countries, primarily in Latin America. Its education program consists of three divisions: The Youth Conservation Program prepares lesson plans and materials for use in Latin American schools. The Public Awareness Program prepares public service ads and films for television and theaters in Latin America; articles for Spanish-language magazines; information pamphlets for the general public; slide shows for public service groups; wildlife films; and poster and button campaigns; and sponsors a lecture series. The Government Information Service develops training and information manuals for local government agencies in Latin America; sponsors a network of U.S. and Latin American agencies to share ideas about conservation problems; and develops ranger training programs.

Recent conservation projects have included, for example, a youth leader training course for Latin Americans, held in Costa Rica; funding a conservation textbook for use in Peruvian schools; production of a film on the Philippine eagle; funding for research on the threatened yellow-tailed woolly monkey of Peru; and a grant to produce a report on the international trade in plants. RARE shares offices with the National Audubon Society and receives "generous logistic support" from Audubon. Its work is supported by contributions from individuals, corporations, and private foundations. Contact: Gerald A. Liberman, President. Pub: Annual report.

RESOURCES FOR THE FUTURE (RFF)
1755 Massachusetts Avenue, N.W.
Washington, D.C. 20036
202-328-5000

RFF is a "private nonprofit organization for research and education in the development, conservation, and use of natural resources and in the improvement of the quality of the environment. Most of RFF's studies are in the social sciences and are broadly concerned with the relationships of people to the natural environment. Specific fields of interest embrace the basic resources of land, water, minerals, and air, and the goods and services derived from them. Special attention is paid to environmental quality, including the relationship of population and economic growth to the environment and resource use in general. Because it is an important factor in every other area, energy is a particularly active concern." RFF was established in 1952 with the cooperation of the Ford Foundation. It has been increasingly interested in international research, especially concerning energy, but also involving forest economics and policy and the management of threats to environmental quality.

Representative recent international projects: energy in developing countries (concentrating on rural electrification, energy demand, and biomass); energy conservation possibilities in Haiti; rural energy development in China; water resource management in Asia; and a workshop on the U.S. international trade in forest products. Contact: Emery N. Castle, President. Pub: RESOURCES, newsletter, three times a year. Numerous books, e.g., U.S. INVESTMENT IN THE FOREST-BASED SECTOR IN LATIN AMERICA (1975); RURAL ENERGY DEVELOPMENT IN CHINA (1982); CHANGING RESOURCE PROBLEMS OF THE FOURTH WORLD (1976). Catalog issued.

SIERRA CLUB
INTERNATIONAL EARTHCARE CENTER
228 E. 45th Street
New York, New York 10017
212-867-0080

The Sierra Club, headquartered in San Francisco, is a major national
conservation organization, founded in 1892. Although the Club was involved in a
limited way in international environmental affairs for many years, its formal
international program dates from 1971, when the Club's board of directors
adopted a resolution stating that "not only is the internationalization of the
environmental movement essential for man's survival, but that very movement
provides the countries of the world with their best chance yet" to improve
international cooperation.

Under a "major new effort to address deteriorating global environmental
conditions," an expanded international program was launched in 1982. The work
of the Club's International Committee and International Earthcare Center will
focus on four areas:

-- Preserving Genetic Diversity. "A campaign to promote protection of
natural areas and genetic diversity worldwide. Included will be tropical
forest and mangrove protection and improved resource management in foreign aid
agencies." This campaign will be guided by a special "Earthcare Committee."

-- Saving Our Seas. "A campaign to implement the environmental protection
standards of the Law of the Sea Treaty, to promote better ocean resource
management, and to safeguard the seas from pollution."

-- Controlling Agrochemical Abuses. "A campaign to control the export and
misuse of pesticides, both to protect human health and species habitat abroad
and to break the 'circle of poison' of pesticides in imported foods.

-- Promoting Caribbean Parks and Preserves. "A Caribbean campaign to make
the United Nations Environment Programme's Caribbean Action Plan effective and
to strengthen citizen environmental groups in the region. Encompassing the
Caribbean islands and coasts from Mexico to Venezuela, we will involve Club
chapters and members with special expertise on island ecology willing to assist
local environmentalists in promoting parks and natural area protection." The
Earthcare Center is currently coordinating a major program, funded by UNEP,
which will generate guidelines for the conservation of mangroves in Trinidad and
Tobago and Venezuela.

Other activities include promoting the implementation of the WORLD CONSERVATION
STRATEGY of the International Union for Conservation of Nature and Natural
Resources; and work on international aspects of acid rain and disposal of
high-level radioactive waste in the oceans.

The Sierra Club's Earthcare Network consists of "a selected group of
environmental organizations which share technical and policy information and
build the intelligence base for the education and training initiatives that are
crucial to sustainable development and global environmental protection. At the
center of international conservation efforts is the range of likeminded
organizations throughout the world which, collectively, can pursue global
environmental goals, such as the Law of the Sea, Antarctica, transboundary air
and water pollution, etc., in the key international treaty forums.

Individually, these groups are powerful allies in seeking conservation legislation within their own countries where it may be inappropriate for the Sierra Club to operate by itself."

Earthcare Network Associates in the U.S. are the Center for Law and Social Policy, East-West Center, Yale University's Forestry and Environmental Studies Library, International Institute for Environment and Development, Natural Resources Defense Council, New York Zoological Society, and The Institute of Ecology. Associates outside the U.S. include groups in Barbados, West Germany, Kenya, Belgium, Venezuela, Ecuador, Indonesia, France, and Costa Rica.

Contact: Patricia J. Scharlin, Director, International Earthcare Center. Pub: Books and reports, e.g., GLOBAL ENERGY IN TRANSITION: ENVIRONMENTAL ASPECTS OF NEW AND RENEWABLE SOURCES FOR DEVELOPMENT (1981); TROPICAL RAINFOREST USE AND PRESERVATION: A STUDY OF PROBLEMS AND PRACTICES IN VENEZUELA (1976). Audiovisual programs on tropical rainforest conservation and ecology theory for planners. Fact sheets and working papers.

STATE UNIVERSITY OF NEW YORK AT BUFFALO
CENTER FOR INTEGRATIVE STUDIES
Hayes Hall, 3435 Main Street
Buffalo, New York 14214
716-831-3727

The Center for Integrative Studies, formerly at the University of Houston, is now part of the School of Architecture and Environmental Design at SUNY Buffalo. Its focus is "on the long range social and cultural implications of change in society, with a strong emphasis on global trends." Aims "are (1) to analyze and project the large scale future consequences of social, cultural, and technological trends in ways that may provide a more holistic framework for their appraisal; (2) to function as a sensing and alerting unit concerned with the effects of changes on the quality of the human environment and with the identification of critical issues which may emerge as focal points for present and future decisions; (3) to explore and formulate guidelines for the study and evaluation of future developments, particularly at the international level, with emphasis on their long range consequences for, and impacts upon, different societies and social groups."

Projects and studies focus on the human environment; world resources and technologies; and emerging human needs and how they might be defined at the global, regional, and local levels, as well as on children's and women's issues. Holds conferences, e.g., International Conference on Bio Resources for Development (Houston, 1978); Future of the Past: Permanence and Change (Mexico City, 1980). Contact: Magda Cordell McHale, Director. Pub: Books, reports, and papers, usually published by other organizations, e.g., WORLD TRENDS AND ALTERNATIVE FUTURES; "Meeting Human Needs within Sustainable Growth;" FACTS AND TRENDS: AN INFORMATION CHARTBOOK.

THRESHOLD, INTERNATIONAL CENTER FOR ENVIRONMENTAL RENEWAL
P.O. Box 4071
Chevy Chase, Maryland 20815
301-654-6570

Threshold, founded in 1972, is an independent, nonprofit organization "serving
to improve mankind's understanding of and relationship to the environment at
five levels: individual/home, neighborhood, city/region, national, and
international." Research, planning, educational, and demonstration activities
work to promote ecologically sound alternatives for practical application, and
focus on energy problems, park planning, and river basin management. Recent
projects have dealt with ecological planning in the Terai region of Nepal;
tropical deforestation; and "development and dissemination of innovative
environmental media on critical international issues." Contact: John P.
Milton, President. Pub: Project reports.

TRAFFIC(U.S.A.)
1601 Connecticut Avenue, N.W.
Washington, D.C. 20009
202-797-7901

"TRAFFIC" is an acronym for Trade Records Analysis of Flora and Fauna in
Commerce. Funded by the World Wildlife Fund-U.S., and part of an international
network of TRAFFIC offices, TRAFFIC(U.S.A.) is a scientific information-
gathering program that monitors national and international trade in wild animals
and plants and the products made from them. Issues reports and presents expert
testimony before U.S. federal and state, international, and foreign government
agencies. Representative recent activities have included investigations of the
tropical fish pet industry; international trade in endangered orchid and cactus
species; exports of U.S. bobcat pelts to Europe; smuggling of exotic birds from
Southeast Asia; and trade in sea turtle products. A particular concern is
monitoring U.S. Government enforcement of its obligations under the Convention
on International Trade in Endangered Species (CITES). Contact: Linda McMahan,
Director. Pub: TRAFFIC(U.S.A.) NEWSLETTER, quarterly. Special Reports, e.g.,
MACAWS: TRADED TO EXTINCTION? (1980); THE INTERNATIONAL TRADE IN PLANTS (1981).
Status Reports, e.g., NEOTROPICAL PSITTACINES IN TRADE (1980). Testimonies,
comments, and presentations.

TRANET
P.O. Box 567
Rangeley, Maine 04970
207-864-2252

TRANET, which stands for "A Transnational Network for Appropriate Technology,"
had its origins at HABITAT: The United Nations Conference on Human Settlements,
held in Vancouver, Canada, in 1976. Its purpose is to stimulate exchanges among
individuals, groups, and networks in all parts of the world who are actively
involved in appropriate technology, or "A.T.", which TRANET defines as "Those
tools, devices, and processes which lead to economic, social, or environmental
improvements by being relatively small scale, low cost, easily maintained,
environmentally sound, and/or resource conserving. They provide creative
employment, raise the quality of life, and increase local self reliance with
optimum use of local resources." TRANET also works to educate the public about

the concepts of A.T., and promotes dialogue towards a reevaluation of the role of science and technology. There are some 450 individual and organizational members. Pub: The main vehicle for carrying out TRANET's work is its quarterly newsletter-directory, TRANET, which lists and describes new and ongoing A.T.-related organizations and activities around the world. It has also issued an INTERNATIONAL DIRECTORY OF APPROPRIATE AND ALTERNATIVE TECHNOLOGY CENTERS.

TUFTS UNIVERSITY
DEPARTMENT OF URBAN AND ENVIRONMENTAL POLICY
Medford, Massachusetts 02155

Held a 14-week experimental course in early 1981, "Global Environmental Strategies in the New England Context," under the auspices of the International Union for Conservation and Natural Resources (IUCN). Its director, Prof. Hermann H. Field, "saw it as a first step in bringing an important 1980 document, the WORLD CONSERVATION STRATEGY, into an educational setting...Because this was a pilot project, it received more attention and resources than is usual for a university course." Speakers included several leading figures in international conservation, e.g., Raymond Dasmann, F. Wayne King, Gerardo Budowski, Kenton R. Miller, Peter Jacobs, Wolfgang Burhenne, and Sidney Holt. The Tufts experience and suggestions for others who may want to prepare similar courses are set forth in a 24-page booklet, "Teaching World Environmental Strategies: One University's Experience," available from Tufts' Department of Urban and Environmental Policy, or from the Commission on Education, IUCN, Avenue du Mont-Blanc, 1196 Gland, Switzerland.

In 1983, Tufts sponsored a gathering at its European Center in France of some 25 corporate executive officers, officers of international funding agencies, representatives of recipient countries, and planning professionals on "environmental planning in the context of development investment." The meeting was the first of a projected series of seminars on key issues of sustainable utilization of global natural resources.

UNIVERSITY OF ARIZONA
OFFICE OF ARID LANDS STUDIES (OALS)
845 N. Park Avenue
Tucson, Arizona 85719
602-626-1955

A major research and information center on the problems of arid regions worldwide. Recent projects have included writing natural resource and environmental profiles of developing countries (sponsored by the U.S. Agency for International Development and the UNESCO Man and the Biosphere Programme); and assisting arid lands research efforts in Saudi Arabia. The Office's Arid Lands Information Center (ALIC) maintains "a unique collection on arid lands of the world. Its emphasis is on the problems and potentials for productive use of arid and semiarid environments." ALIC compiles a major monthly journal, ARID LANDS ABSTRACTS, published by the Commonwealth Agricultural Bureaux (Farnham Royal, Slough SL2 3BN, England). Customized reference service uses on-line bibliographic searching. The Office's Rapid Reconnaissance Service is a "geographic information service for rural development practitioners needing Landsat imagery, maps, area profiles, and other information on developing countries. Plans a major international conference in October 1985, "Land-Use Systems in Arid and Semiarid Regions." Pub: ARID LANDS NEWSLETTER, semiannual magazine. Reports; conference proceedings; information papers.

UNIVERSITY OF DELAWARE
CENTER FOR THE STUDY OF MARINE POLICY
Robinson Hall 301
Newark, Delaware 19711
302-738-8086

Recent projects have included studies of the physical, political, legal, and economic aspects of the key narrows (international straits) of the world ocean; the energy policies of selected coastal countries; and the law of the sea. Contact: Gerard J. Mangone, Director. Pub: MARINE POLICY REPORTS, five times a year.

UNIVERSITY OF MICHIGAN
SCHOOL OF NATURAL RESOURCES
Ann Arbor, Michigan 48109
313-763-2200

Since the early 1970s, the University of Michigan's School of Natural Resources has had an active program in international aspects of natural resource management. In addition to holding courses and seminars for its own students, the School has also conducted a number of research and training projects in collaboration with international and foreign organizations. In 1981, the School established the Center for Strategic Wildland Management Studies, also known as the Wildland Management Center (WMC), to bring together its resources on "important global issues involving the protection and use of wild species and natural ecosystems for sustainable development."

WMC field actions and research activities center on six themes: (1) identifying and managing critical natural areas; (2) ensuring sustainable utilization of renewable resources; (3) incorporating ecological principles into development planning; (4) exploring values associated with natural area management; (5) furthering awareness of the relationship of natural resources to human welfare; and (6) developing the capacity to manage natural resources. Recent field activities have focused on Latin America and the Caribbean. WMC also collaborates directly with the International Union for Conservation of Nature and Natural Resources (IUCN); participates in the cooperative Eastern Caribbean Natural Area Management Program (ECNAMP); and exchanges students with the Tropical Agricultural Research and Training Center (CATIE) in Turrialba, Costa Rica.

The School of Natural Resources has also sponsored an annual International Seminar on National Parks and Equivalent Reserves, in cooperation with the U.S. National Park Service and Parks Canada. The month-long seminar, designed for senior administrators, professional personnel, and conservation leaders responsible for the establishment and management of park and wildlife conservation systems, has been attended by over 500 persons from nearly 100 countries.

UNIVERSITY OF MINNESOTA
HUBERT H. HUMPHREY INSTITUTE OF PUBLIC AFFAIRS
Social Sciences Building
612-373-2653

The Humphrey Institute's Global Environmental Policy Project "represents a major inquiry into the implications of the global warming of the atmosphere...This buildup of carbon dioxide in the atmosphere is now regarded by some experts as a prime environmental risk demanding either preventive or adaptive actions of enormous scale and difficulty." The Institute held a national conference on the subject in 1981, and has published its proceedings. Contact: Dean E. Abrahamson, Director, Global Environmental Policy Project.

UNIVERSITY OF NEW MEXICO SCHOOL OF LAW
NATURAL RESOURCES CENTER
Albuquerque, New Mexico 87131

Has a continuing interest in international environmental problems, especially from a legal standpoint. Publishes NATURAL RESOURCES JOURNAL, quarterly, which frequently includes articles on international legal issues in the field. Environmental management problems in the Mexico-U.S. border area have been a special interest. A "Symposium on U.S.-Mexican Transboundary Resources" was published in the October 1977 number of NATURAL RESOURCES JOURNAL. An international workshop, "Anticipating Transboundary Resource Needs and Issues," was held in 1981, from which resulteda report, SELECTED RESOURCE ISSUES IN THE BORDER REGION. Contact: Albert E. Utton, Director.

UNIVERSITY OF NORTH CAROLINA
SCHOOL OF PUBLIC HEALTH
DEPARTMENT OF ENVIRONMENTAL SCIENCES AND ENGINEERING
Rosenau Hall 201 H
Chapel Hill, North Carolina 27514
919-966-3751

The Department of Environmental Health and Engineering has undertaken projects on behalf of the U.S. Agency for International Development (USAID) and its predecessor agencies continuously since 1954, and with the sponsorship of the World Health Organization, World Bank, and other international organizations. These have included designing and conducting courses and seminars at universities in developing countries, as well as in the U.S. for participants from developing countries. For five years in the 1970s, it conducted the International Program on the Environmental Aspects of Industrial Development (IPEAID) on the Chapel Hill campus for governmental officials from many developing countries. Currently, the Department conducts the Environmental Training and Management in Africa (ETMA) project, in cooperation with Clark University and the South-East Consortium for International Development. ETMA provides environmental training seminars and courses in African countries and also offers technical assistance in environmental resource management. The Department also participates in the USAID-sponsored Water and Sanitation for Health (WASH) project, which provides information, technical help, and training to improve drinking water and sanitation in developing countries.

UNIVERSITY OF VIRGINIA
CENTER FOR OCEAN LAW AND POLICY
School of Law
Charlottesville, Virginia 22901
804-924-7441

Founded in 1976, the Center is concerned with "the future of the oceans, coastal and polar areas and the decisions which affect their use and protection...and seeks to assist in promoting rational choices for managing these areas through teaching, research, and the dissemination of information. Ocean choices of concern to the Center are presented at every decision level: international, national, regional, state, and local." Interests include such international issues as vessel source pollution, Arctic policy, and the law of the sea. Contact: John Norton Moore, Director. Pub: OCEAN POLICY STUDIES, annual volumes of 6-8 studies.

U.S. ASSOCIATION FOR THE CLUB OF ROME (USACOR)
1735 DeSales Street, N.W.
Washington, D.C. 20036
202-638-1029

The Club of Rome is an unusual organization that was founded in 1968 by Italian industrialist and economist Aurelio Peccei, who began by bringing together 30 people from ten countries - scientists, educators, economists, humanists, industrialists, and national and international civil servants - to "discuss a subject of immense scope: the present and future predicament of mankind." The Club itself is limited to no more than 100 members. Its objectives are "to promote and disseminate a more secure, in-depth understanding of mankind's predicament...and to stimulate the adoption of new attitudes, policies, and institutions capable of redressing the present situation." Its first project resulted in publication of the widely-publicized study, THE LIMITS TO GROWTH (1970), which concluded that if present growth trends in world population, industrialization, food production, and resource depletion continue unchanged, the limits to growth on this planet will be reached sometime within the next 100 years. It also concluded that it is possible to alter these growth trends and to establish a condition of ecological and economic stability that is sustainable far into the future.

Since publication of THE LIMITS TO GROWTH, the Club of Rome has sponsored and published eight additional studies: MANKIND AT THE TURNING POINT (1974); RESHAPING THE INTERNATIONAL ORDER ("RIO," 1976); GOALS FOR MANKIND (1977); BEYOND THE AGE OF WASTE (1978); ENERGY: THE COUNTDOWN (1979); NO LIMITS TO LEARNING (1979); DIALOGUE ON WEALTH AND WELFARE (1980); and ROAD MAPS TO THE FUTURE (1980). All were published commercially and are available through bookstores.

"The Club of Rome is continuing its activities much as before, but in recent years its activities have been augmented by a growing number of affiliated national organizations and associations. Since the Club of Rome is itself a non-organization [Peccei's idea was that the Club should operate on the leanest budget possible and work through the many organizations already in existence], its ties to the national organizations are informal and philosophical, rather than administrative, legal, or financial. Aurelio Peccei provides the principal linkage through his frequent travels, reports, letters, and telephone calls."

The U.S. Association for the Club of Rome is one of 14 such national affiliates.
(The others are in Australia, Belgium, Canada, Finland, Greece, Japan, the
Netherlands, New Zealand, Spain, Switzerland, Turkey, the United Kingdom, and
West Germany.) Formed in 1976, it acts "primarily as a catalyst of ideas. It
is not a mass-membership, lobbying group, and has no aspirations to become one.
USACOR will remain small. It was initially limited to 100 members. It is now
expanding its membership to 500 so as to be more nationally representative."
Membership, which is highly selective and must be approved by the organization's
board of directors, is for a term of three years, and can be renewed. Members
include many of the American leaders and thinkers most prominent in working on
global problems.

The U.S. association's activities include periodic membership meetings, usually
in Washington, D.C., an informal newsletter issued 6-8 times a year, public
conferences from time to time, and dissemination of studies and reports. "The
basic objectives of these activities are (1) to help disseminate information
about the interlinkage of complex global problems, and the role and
responsibility of the United States in these problems; (2) to stimulate
discussion of creative policy alternatives for the future as a first step toward
timely and appropriate public decisions in the United States; and (3) to provide
a network of information, support, and personal encouragement for members as
well as others in the United States who share similar concerns and interests."

Contact: Faye Beuby, Executive Director. Pub: NEWSLETTER, 6-8 times a year.
Occasional reports and papers. Publications are available to non-members on a
subscription basis. MAKING IT HAPPEN: A POSITIVE GUIDE TO THE FUTURE, by John
M. Richardson, Jr., 1982.

WHALE CENTER
3929 Piedmont Avenue
Oakland, California 94611
415-654-6621

Goals are "to end commercial whaling, establish a global system of
internationally recognized whale sanctuaries, and increase research and
understanding of living whales." Current and recent international activities
have included developing a proposed international plan to ensure survival of the
gray whale, with governmental officials and experts from the U.S., USSR, Canada,
and Mexico; monitoring meetings of the International Whaling Commission;
research on the gray whale in Mexico; and participating in coalitions of groups
concerned with such international issues as the Law of the Sea, the Convention
on International Trade in Endangered Species (CITES), the Migratory Species
Convention, and the future of Antarctica and the Southern Ocean. Serves as the
headquarters of Whale Centers International, which is a member of the
International Union for Conservation of Nature and Natural Resources (IUCN).
Contact: Maxine McCloskey, Executive Director. Pub: WHALE CENTER NEWSLETTER,
2-4 times a year. WHALE CENTER BULLETIN, irregular. Reprints of articles;
educational materials for school children.

WILDLIFE PRESERVATION TRUST INTERNATIONAL, INC. (WPTI)
34th Street and Girard Avenue
Philadelphia, Pennsylvania 19104
215-222-3636

Founded by Gerald Durrell in 1971, the Wildlife Preservation Trust works to preserve threatened and endangered animal species through captive propagation and by advancing the science of animal propagation. The Trust consists of two units, an operating foundation on the English Channel island of Jersey, and a granting foundation, WPTI, based in Philadelphia. The Trust "generally restricts its attention to vertebrates (and principally terrestrial ones) which are some of the more intricate and behaviorally complex of animals, and consequently often among the first species to be imperiled in the course of pressure on the wilderness. The Trust considers reintroduction of animals to the wild to be part of its responsibility, at least in terms of providing stock and developing the scientific basis for introduction." Recent and current projects have been concerned with such species as the Japanese crested ibis, parrots on the Caribbean island of St. Lucia, the snow leopard of Central Asia, and the lowland gorillas of Africa. Operates an International Training Center in Jersey. Contact: Jon M. Jensen, Executive Director. Pub: ON THE EDGE, semiannual newsletter. THE DODO, an annual technical journal published in Jersey.

THE WILDLIFE SOCIETY
5410 Grosvenor Lane
Bethesda, Maryland 20814
301-897-9770

Founded in 1937, The Wildlife Society is a professional, nonprofit organization "dedicated to the wise management and conservation of the wildlife resources of the world. Ecology is the primary scientific discipline of the wildlife profession. The interests of the Society, therefore, embrace the interactions of all organisms with their natural environments." The membership of some 10,000 is composed of research scientists, educators, communications specialists, conservation law enforcement officials, resource managers, and administrators from over 70 countries. The main focus is on North America, but the Society periodically holds international conferences and workshops (e.g., International Congress of Game Biologists, Atlanta, 1977; workshop in India on wildlife management techniques in Asia, 1982). Contact: Harry E. Hodgdon, Executive Director. Pub: THE JOURNAL OF WILDLIFE MANAGEMENT, quarterly. WILDLIFE SOCIETY BULLETIN, quarterly. Books, special publications, texts, and reference books.

WOODS HOLE OCEANOGRAPHIC INSTITUTION (WHOI)
Woods Hole, Massachusetts 02543
617-548-1400

Woods Hole is an independent, major national marine research organization that conducts studies in biology, chemistry, geology and geophysics, ocean engineering, and physical oceanography, as well as marine policy and management. The Marine Policy and Ocean Management Program (MPOM) is a "multidisciplinary effort that provides an opportunity for individual scholars to conduct research regarding the problems generated by man's increasing use of the ocean." The

Program sponsors workshops, conferences, and seminars on "important and timely marine policy issues." In addition to work on domestic coastal management, marine pollution, and fisheries issues, the Program has a project on Cooperative International Marine Policy, which "considers the transfer of marine science and technology to developing countries for the purpose of marine resource management." Research involves "the design of a mechanism for identifying countries interested in this kind of assistance and implementation of training modules in the form of mini-courses and workshops."

Contact: David A. Ross, Director, Marine Policy and Ocean Management Program. Pub: Papers published in scientific journals (annual list available).

WORLD ENVIRONMENT CENTER
605 Third Avenue
New York, New York 10158
212-986-7200

Organized in 1974 at the request of the United Nations Environment Programme (UNEP) and in cooperation with the United Nations Association of the U.S.A. Original purpose was to increase public understanding in North America of international environment and development issues and how they relate to natural resource management in Canada and the U.S. In practice, a wider audience has developed and information now goes to policy makers in over 50 countries.

Holds conferences, e.g., on the environmental practices of consulting firms working in international development. Grants annual International Environmental Award, on World Environment Day, to an individual or institution that has made a significant contribution to increasing understanding of issues or to environmental management as applied to international development. Contact: Whitman Bassow, President.

Pub: WORLD ENVIRONMENT REPORT, biweekly newsletter covering environmental trends and developments in some 100 countries; subscription ($120.00 per year) includes access to Center's information resources. Directories, including THE WORLD ENVIRONMENT HANDBOOK (a directory of government natural resource management agencies in 144 countries); CONTACT: TOXICS — A GUIDE TO SPECIALISTS ON TOXIC SUBSTANCES; and CONTACT: ENERGY — A GUIDE TO ENERGY SPECIALISTS. Reports, including ENVIRONMENTAL TRAINING IN DEVELOPING COUNTRIES; and a series, ENVIRONMENTAL DEVELOPMENTS IN THE WORLD'S MAJOR GEOGRAPHIC REGIONS. Conference proceedings.

WORLD FUTURE SOCIETY
4916 St. Elmo Avenue
Washington, D.C. 20014
202-656-8274

An "association of people who are interested in how social and technological developments will shape the future," with some 50,000 members in over 80 countries. Publications frequently discuss and describe information resources on problems and opportunities related to the global environment. Major conferences have included "The Next 25 Years: Crisis and Opportunity" (Washington, 1975) and the First Global Conference on the Future (Toronto, 1980). Contact: Edward S. Cornish, President and Editor.

Pub: THE FUTURIST, bimonthly magazine; newsletters; books; conference tapes; source guides (including THE FUTURE: A GUIDE TO INFORMATION SOURCES, periodically revised).

WORLD RESOURCES INSTITUTE (WRI)
1735 New York Avenue, N.W.
Washington, D.C. 20006
202-638-6300

Launched in the fall of 1982 with a grant from the John D. and Catherine T. MacArthur Foundation, the World Resources Institute is a major new center for policy research "that seeks to address a fundamental question: how can the world's people and nations meet their basic needs and economic requirements without at the same time undermining the earth's ability to provide the natural resources and environmental quality on which life, growth, and security depend?

"The World Resources Institute brings together leading thinkers from many fields and countries to study these questions and to create policy options for the difficult choices that lie ahead. The Institute is independent, not-for-profit, and nonpartisan. It is concerned with the constructive involvement of private companies and other national and international organizations as well as with governmental decisions. Its approach is objective and open-minded -- but not neutral; it is committed to the search for more knowledge as a basis for better decisions as a basis for better decisions on global issues of great importance.

"The Institute carries out a variety of activities. Through its research, it aims to provide accurate information about global resources and environmental conditions, analysis of emerging issues, and development of creative yet workable policy responses. In seeking to deepen public understanding, it publishes a variety of reports and papers, undertakes briefings, seminars, and conferences, and offers material for use in the press and on the air. It works with government officials and private sector leaders in the U.S. and abroad. A central task of the Institute is to build bridges between scholarship and policy, bringing together the insights of scientific research, economic analysis, and experienced policy judgment."

The "distinctive character" of the World Resources Institute is in its "global perspective, broad participation, and policy relevance."

-- Global perspective. "The Institute explores world-scale natural resoure and environmental issues, including their relation to population, and not issues of local or national significance only. Of course, subjects of special concern to one country, such as U.S. agricultural production, can be of worldwide importance."

-- Broad participation. "The Institute seeks to involve many communities -- government, science, business, conservationist, labor, and others -- in its program and acts as a center for the exchange of information, ideas, and viewpoints. Building from a strong base in the natural sciences, the Institute insists on an interdisciplinary approach, including economics and other social sciences, in its investigations. This approach is reflected in its staff and fellows program which bring together experts from many fields. The Institute enjoys an unusual relationship with affiliated institutions across the country and abroad. These affiliates are established centers of excellence, in universities and elsewhere, whose members work with and contribute to the work

of the Institute's Washington center. Through this 'hub and spokes'
arrangement, members of the affiliated institutions can play a stronger role in
the policy deliberations of government and private organizations."

-- Policy relevance. "The Institute seeks to address issues that are, or
should be, policy issues and does so in a way that is useful to policy makers.
The Institute's research concentrates on developing policy options and analyzing
their benefits, costs, and feasibility. Timing, accessible presentation, use of
nontechnical language, and the follow-up that injects research findings into the
process of actually making decisions are important considerations. The
Institute is not a lobby or pressure group, but it works to ensure that its
findings and conclusions are brought to the attention of those in government,
business, and elsewhere who might find them useful."

In mid-1983, the Institute planned to undertake the following projects during
the 1983-85 period:

-- Program in Living Resources. This program covers the subject of
biological resources, their use and depletion. The main project planned is
"Biological Diversity," which will be concerned with the accelerating loss of
species. Research in this area "would synthesize what is known about the
dimensions of species loss; analyze what such losses are likely to mean to
mankind...investigate the causes of species loss, and identify and assess
policies that can improve the current situation, with particular emphasis on
economic incentives and institutional mechanisms to promote conservation in the
developing countries where most species exist and where most are lost. The
research would focus initially on tropical forests, the microbial world, and
marine coral reefs."

-- Program in Agricultural Resources. "Research in this area will focus on
the means to conserve or improve the resources necessary for food production,
including: preservation of agricultural lands, conservation and enhancement of
productive soils, efficient management of water resources, development of
appropriate genetic strategies, and wise use of agrochemicals." Projects
already planned are "Desertification in North America" and "Agricultural Land
Transformation." The latter project, to be undertaken jointly with the
Scientific Committee on Problems of the Environment of the International Council
of Scientific Unions (SCOPE), will be an "international study of the
transformation (degradation, improvement, and conversion) of agricultural
lands."

-- Program in Energy, Climate, and Industrial Resources. "This program
concentrates on the economic, social, political and, of course, the
environmental and resource implications of alternative global energy futures and
policies." Projected projects include "Global Energy Futures," "Carbon Dioxide
and Climate Change," "Methanol," and "Solar Energy and Development."

-- Program in Pollution and Health. "This program will investigate
management and prevention strategies for forms of pollution of the transnational
type, including acid precipitation, hazardous substances, radioactive or toxic
wastes, and automobile pollution. It will also address issues such as the
health and environmental effects of biocidal and other chemicals, sanitation,
and water and airborne diseases." The first project planned in this area is
"Global Pesticide Use."

-- Program in Information, Institutions, and Governance. "This program focuses on the most valuable resource -- information -- and on the social, political, and economic forces that shape policy. It deals with the identification and assessment of global conditions, trends, and prospects, and with the adequacy of available data for both documentation and forecasting. It is also concerned with the means to put both information and financial resources to better practical use, through improving access to data and expertise, and creating the necessary governmental, private sector, and other policies. It will consider the adequacy of existing institutional means for reaching international consensus and for taking cooperative action." Projects in this area will include THE WORLD RESOURCES REPORT, an annual volume produced by WRI and the International Institute for Environment and Development (IIED). This will consist of essays; an annual review of events, trends, and research; and a presentation of global data and statistics. Other projects will include "Private Sector Initiatives" (to "explore areas of high mutual interest to WRI and to the business community"); "The Global Possible: A Positive View of the Future" (a conference to "identify concrete, feasible ways to achieve the best possible management of the global environment and to portray the global future as it might look under these circumstances"); and "The U.S. Stake in Global Issues" ("to explore, define, and communicate the longer-term U.S. political, economic, and security stake in global resource, environmental, population, and related development issues").

Contact: J. Gustave Speth, President.

WORLDWATCH INSTITUTE
1776 Massachusetts Avenue, N.W.
Washington, D.C. 20036
202-452-1999

Worldwatch is an independent, nonprofit research organization created in 1974 to "alert policymakers and the general public to emerging global trends in the availability and managament of resources - both human and natural. The research program is designed to fill the gap left by traditional analyses in providing the information needed by decision makers in today's rapidly changing and interdependent world. Worldwatch analyzes issues in a global perspective and within an interdisciplinary framework." The primary vehicle for disseminating information is a series of Worldwatch Papers and books. Results of the Institute's research projects are also published widely in scholarly and popular periodicals. Contact: Lester R. Brown, President. Pub: Worldwatch Papers; 54 of these had been issued by June 1983. Examples in the field of environmnental and natural resource management: ELECTRICITY FROM SUNLIGHT: THE FUTURE OF PHOTOVOLTAICS; SIX STEPS TO A SUSTAINABLE SOCIETY; RIVERS OF ENERGY: THE HYDROPOWER POTENTIAL; WOOD: AN ANCIENT FUEL WITH A NEW FUTURE; FOOD OR FUEL: NEW COMPETITION FOR THE WORLD'S CROPLAND; RESOURCE TRENDS AND POPULATION POLICY: A TIME FOR REASSESSMENT. Worldwatch books, issued by commercial publishers, e.g., THE TWENTY-NINTH DAY: ACCOMODATING HUMAN NEEDS AND NUMBERS TO THE EARTH'S RESOURCES (1978); THE PICTURE OF HEALTH: ENVIRONMENTAL SOURCES OF DISEASE (1977). Papers and books are sold individually or by annual subscription.

WORLD WILDLIFE FUND-U.S. (WWF-US)
1601 Connecticut Avenue, N.W.
Washington, D.C. 20009
202-387-0800

World Wildlife Fund International, headquartered in Gland, Switerland, was
founded in 1961 with the primary purpose of providing financial support to
conservation programs of the International Union for Conservation of Nature and
Natural Resources (IUCN). WWF International "has spent more than $65 million on
some 3000 projects in 130 countries and has helped create or support 260
national parks on five continents, a total area nearly twice the size of Texas,
and has helped rescue many threatened or endangered species from extinction."
WWF has 24 affiliated national organizations, of which WWF-US is one.

WWF-US raised $5.7 million in the fiscal year that ended June 30, 1982. "While
continuing to be the largest single private source in the U.S. of grants for
international conservation work by institutions and individuals, WWF-US is also
an independent conservation organization in its own right with a significant
presence in the United States. With a strong professional staff, WWF-US has
developed its own long-term projects on the conservation of tropical forests,
the conservation of primates and migratory birds, the establishment of parks and
other protected areas, and the intensive monitoring of trade in wildlife and
wildlife products through U.S. ports of entry."

WWF-US also supports international conservation programs of other organizations,
e.g., the Environmental Defense Fund and Natural Resources Defense Council, and
it has jointly funded projects with such organizations as the Smithsonian
Institution, National Geographic Society, Nature Conservancy, New York
Zoological Society, New York Botanic Garden, and African Wildlife Foundation.

WWF-US projects are divided into 8 areas:

    -- Tropical Forests. The highest priority of WWF-US since 1974, work in
this area includes projects on tropical forests and climate (focusing on what
combination of land uses are permissible in the Amazon Basin to protect the
integrity of the forest-rainfall relationship); the minimum critical size of
ecosystems (concerned with the problem of what size and shape national parks and
other protected areas should be to protect natural communities); eastern
Brazil; ethnobotany in South America; and the tropical forest industry.

    -- Marine Ecosystems. The goal of this program is "the maintenance of a
rational, sustainable relationship between man and marine life. WWF-US selects
projects which promote the conservation of endangered species, the sustainable
use of marine resources, and identification and protection of critical habitat."
In this area, work concentrates on conservation of sea turtles, whales, and
fisheries.

    -- Endangered and Migratory Species. This program includes work on the
protection of migratory birds, focusing on the Western Hemisphere; support for
captive breeding of the Siberian crane; support for the International Council
for Bird Preservation; contributions to IUCN's RED DATA BOOKS, which contain
current information on the status of threatened wild animals and plants; and
work on protection of giant pandas, freshwater turtles, and anti-poaching of
African mammals.

-- Primates. WWF-US has helped to develop, fund, and implement some 60 primate conservation projects in 25 countries, most of them aimed at either ensuring the survival of particular endangered and vulnerable species or providing effective protection for large numbers of primates in areas of high primate diversity or abundance. Major projects focus on Brazil, Madagascar, Central Africa, Indonesia, and South Asia. Support is also given for work on trade in living nonhuman primates and to the Duke University Primate Center.

-- Parks and Protection of Habitat. "Since 1961, WWF-US has helped to set aside, plan, manage, and equip literally millions of acres rich in biological resources." Current projects focus on the Western Hemisphere, particularly Colombia, Costa Rica, and the Caribbean region, and the African country of Sierra Leone. The Fund also supports PARKS MAGAZINE, the only international journal on park planning and management for professionals.

-- Training and Conservation Education. "The greatest obstacles to effective conservation efforts in developing countries are the lack of trained professionals in the fields of wildlife and natural resource management and the lack of awareness of the long term benefits of sound conservation policies. WWF-US is addressing these policies in a number of ways: (1) providing fellowships to short training courses for park and wildlife personnel; (2) training graduate students and scientists as a part of WWF-US funded research projects; and (3) including conservation education and public awareness programs in projects whenever possible." WWF-US also gives financial support to the International Seminar on National Parks at the University of Michigan, and to the Earthscan program of the International Institute for Environment and Development (IIED).

-- TRAFFIC(U.S.A.). This organization, described separately in this book, receives most of its funding from WWF-US.

-- Development of Conservation Policy. "WWF-US staff fund or work with other organizations, both public and private, and help to mobilize scientific expertise in formulating and implementing coordinated, comprehensive public conservation policy." Recent efforts in this area have included working for reauthorization of the U.S. Endangered Species Act, an international strategy conference on biological diversity, and funding for policy projects of the International Union for Conservation of Nature and Natural Resources (IUCN), Natural Resources Defense Fund, Environmental Defense Fund, and the international Scientific Committee on Problems of the Environment (SCOPE).

Contact: Russell E. Train, President. WWF-US maintains a New York office at 100 Park Avenue, New York, N.Y. 10017, telephone 212-889-8006. Pub: FOCUS, bi-monthly newspaper.

ZOOLOGICAL SOCIETY OF SAN DIEGO
P.O. Box 551
San Diego, California 92112
916-231-1515

Operates one of the world's major zoos, as well as a large rural animal park. The Society's International Center for Reproduction of Endangered Species is a long-range, in-house research program for reproduction of endangered animal species in captivity. Has hosted major conferences on international conservation topics. Pub: ZOONOOZ, monthly. Newsletter, quarterly. Contact: Marvin Jones, Registrar.

INDEX

National Parks and Conservation
  Assn, 47
National Park Service, 12
National Research Council, 47
National Resources Defense Council,
  48
National Wildlife Federation, 50
National Zoological Park, 20
Nature Conservancy, 50
New York Zoological Society, 51
Nuclear Regulatory Commission, 19
Oceanic Society, 51
Ocean Policy Committee, NRC, 48
Ocean Sciences Board, NRC, 48
Ocean Search Expeditions, 32
Office of Arid Lands Studies, 57
Office of Biological Conservation,
  Smithsonian, 20
Office of International Fisheries
  Affairs, 10
Office of International Science, AAAS,
  23
Office of Marine Mammals and
  Endangered Species, 10
Office of Technology Assessment, 7
Pacific Islands Forestry Information
  Center, 10
Pacific Seabird Group, 52
Peace Corps, 19
Polar Research Board, NRC, 48
Project Jonah, 52
Rachael Carson Council, 52
Rapid Reconnaissance Service, 57
RARE, Inc., 53
Research Materials Center, East-West
  Center, 35
Resources for the Future, 53
Scientific Activities Overseas
  program, EPA, 18
Sierra Club, 54
Smithsonian Institution, 20
Smithsonian Tropical Research
  Institute, 20
State University of New York at
  Buffalo, 55
Threshold, 56
Traffic(U.S.A.), 56
TRANET, 56
Tufts University, 57
United States or U.S. (government
  agencies): See next word in title.
U.S. Association for the Club of
  Rome, 60
U.S.-Egypt Joint Consultative
  Committee, 48

U.S.-Japan Cooperative Program on
  Nature and Natural Resources, 14
U.S.-Mexico Joint Committee on
  Wildlife Conservation, 13
University of Arizona, 57
University of Delaware, 58
University of Hawaii, 44
University of Michigan, 58
University of Minnesota, 59
University of New Mexico, 59
University of North Carolina, 59
University of Virginia, 60
Water and Sanitation for Health, 59
Western Hemisphere Cooperation
  Project, 23
Whale Center, 61
Wildland Management Center, 58
Wildlife Preservation Trust
  International, 62
Wildlife Society, 62
Woods Hole Oceanographic Institution,
  62
"World Conservation Strategy," 43
World Environment Center, 63
World Future Society, 63
World Resources Institute, 64
Worldwatch Institute, 66
World Wildlife Fund, 67
Zoological Society of San Diego, 68

INDEX OF ACRONYMS AND INITIALISMS

AAAS, 23
AALS, 27
AAZPA, 24
ACIC, 25
AC/ICSU, 48
ACS, 24
AID, 15
ALIC, 57
APA, 25
API, 25
BNA, 27
BOSTID, 47
CAES, 28
CDRI, 30
CEQ, 7
CF, 31
CIPA, 28
CITES, 14
CLASP, 29
CODEL, 32
CRC, 20

SELECTED PUBLICATIONS OF
THE CALIFORNIA INSTITUTE OF PUBLIC AFFAIRS
ON ENVIRONMENTAL AND NATURAL RESOURCE PROBLEMS

Reference Books — National and International:

Energy: A Guide to Organizations and Information Resources in the United States. Second Edition, 1978.

World Directory of Environmental Organizations. Published for the Sierra Club in cooperation with the International Union for Conservation of Nature and Natural Resources. Second Edition, 1976.

Population: An International Directory of Organizations and Information Resources, 1977.

World Food Crisis: An International Directory of Organizations and Information Resources, 1977.

Urban Mass Transit: A Guide to Organizations and Information Resources, 1979.

The Nuclear Power Issue: A Guide to Who's Doing What in the U.S. and Abroad, 1981.

The United States and the Global Environment: A Guide to American Organizations Concerned with International Environmental Issues, 1983.

Reference Books — California:

California Environmental Directory: A Guide to Organizations and Resources. Third Edition, 1980.

California Energy Directory: A Guide to Organizations and Information Resources, 1980.

California Water Resources Directory: A Guide to Organizations and Information Resources, 1983.

California Farmlands Project:

Preserving Agricultural Lands: An International Annotated Bibliography, 1983.

How Can Land Be Saved for Agriculture? Proceedings of a Working Conference to Find Solutions for California, 1983.

Agricultural Land Preservation in California: An Overview, 1982.

Local Farmlands Protection in California: Studies of Problems, Programs, and Policies in Seven Counties, 1983.

Issues and Alternatives: Reasons and Methods for Protecting California Farmlands, 1983.

Write for a complete descriptive list of our publications.

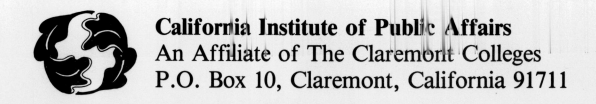

California Institute of Public Affairs
An Affiliate of The Claremont Colleges
P.O. Box 10, Claremont, California 91711